ONCE UPON A RHYME

IMAGINATION FOR A NEW GENERATION

Wales Vol II
Edited by Kelly Oliver

First published in Great Britain in 2004 by:
Young Writers
Remus House
Coltsfoot Drive
Peterborough
PE2 9JX
Telephone: 01733 890066
Website: www.youngwriters.co.uk

All Rights Reserved

© Copyright Contributors 2004

SB ISBN 1 84460 533 7

Foreword

Young Writers was established in 1991 and has been passionately devoted to the promotion of reading and writing in children and young adults ever since. The quest continues today. Young Writers remains as committed to engendering the fostering of burgeoning poetic and literary talent as ever.

This year's Young Writers competition has proven as vibrant and dynamic as ever and we are delighted to present a showcase of the best poetry from across the UK. Each poem has been carefully selected from a wealth of *Once Upon A Rhyme* entries before ultimately being published in this, our twelfth primary school poetry series.

Once again, we have been supremely impressed by the overall high quality of the entries we have received. The imagination, energy and creativity which has gone into each young writer's entry made choosing the best poems a challenging and often difficult but ultimately hugely rewarding task - the general high standard of the work submitted amply vindicating this opportunity to bring their poetry to a larger appreciative audience.

We sincerely hope you are pleased with our final selection and that you will enjoy *Once Upon A Rhyme Wales Vol II* for many years to come.

Contents

Lucy Webb (9)	1
Lily May Usher (12)	2

Ciliau Parc Primary School, Lampeter
Owen Rose (11)	3
Rose Darlington (10)	4
Aimee Hughes (10)	4
Tom Wolfe (9)	5
Lauren Upshall (10)	5
Ruby Wakley (9)	6
Morgan Davies (10)	7

Crossgates Primary School, Llandrindod Wells
Sarah Powell (10)	7
George Williams (10)	8
Rhiannon Lewis (11)	9
Andrea Burton (11)	9
Annie Morris (11)	10
Rosie Stephens (11)	10
Matthew Jones (11)	11
Emma Collins (10)	12
Gary Pritchard (11)	12
Kashika Paris (10)	13
Nathan Dunn (10)	13
Curtis Leavesley (11)	14
Evie Doman (11)	14

Forden CW Primary School, Welshpool
Gareth Morgan (11)	15
Megan Dyer (10)	15
Fabian Twist (11)	16

Guilsfield CP School, Welshpool
Alex Charlesworth (9)	16
Danielle Pearce (8)	17
Henry Richards (10)	18
Bethany Dodd (10)	19

Abbie Knight (10)	20
Rhys Jones (11)	20
Katie Davies (10)	21
Jessica Thomas (10)	22
Gwynnfore Evans (11)	23

Haverfordwest VC School, Haverfordwest

Ellen Banner (8)	24
Jacob Thomas (8)	24
Elin Newton (8)	25
Thomas Easton (8)	25
Danielle Thomas (8)	26
Joshua Ward (8)	26
Kirsty Lewis (7)	27
Luke Eden (8)	27
Jessica James (7)	28
Richard Thomas (7)	28
Alex Roberts (8)	29
Lucy Campbell (7)	29
Tommy-Lee Vores (8)	29
Jessica Davies (10)	30
Bethan Hoare (8)	30
Carli Absalom (8)	31
Emily Pemberthy (8)	31
Jacob Arnold (8)	32
Joe Lloyd (9)	32
Leanne John (8)	33
Louise Morris (8)	33
Lucas Horton (8)	34
Roxanne Griffiths (8)	34
Rhys Morris (8)	35
Ryan Wilson (9)	35
Ryan Scott & Rhys Thomas (8)	36
Connor Nurse (8)	36
Tommy Bolstridge Edwards (8)	36

Hendy-Gwyn Primary School, Whitland

Sophie Russell (10)	37
Eilesha Clarke (10)	37
Lucy Duncombe (11)	37
Ella Storer (10)	37

Jasmine Sterndale (10) — 38
Josef Watson (9) — 38
Nikita Evans (10) — 38
Daniel Chick (10) — 38
Kyle Naylor (11) — 39
Sophie Jackson (11) — 39

Lakefield Primary School, Llanelli
Daniel Benjamin (10) — 40
Shaldon Hayes (9) — 40
Ben Davies (10) — 41
Lewis Williams (10) — 41
Jake Rees (11) — 42
Carly McCann (10) — 42
Adam Entwistle (10) — 43
Ainsley Brown (9) — 43
Alanna James (10) — 44
Chloe Thomas (10) — 44
Bethany Nicholas (9) — 45
Jessica Colwill (10) — 45
Alex Mears (10) — 45
Sophie Hope (10) — 46
Georgia Shephard (8) — 46
Lucy Green (9) — 47
Andreas Taffetsauffer (8) — 47
Ashley Copeman (9) — 48
Annelise Davies (9) — 49
Heather Hurt (8) — 49
Gemma Williams (9) — 49
Charlotte Morrison (9) — 50
Jessica Withers (8) — 50
Carys James (9) — 50
Liam Green (7) — 51
Siân Jones-Higginson (8) — 51
Rubell Khan (8) — 52
Jordan Howe (8) — 52
Holly Ann Yeo (8) — 53
Jordan Lewis (8) — 53
Thomas Parry (7) — 54
Emily Prentice-Gregory (10) — 54
Rebecca Bello (10) — 55

Stacey Evans (10)	55
Jack Rolfe (8)	56
Alysha Gibson (11)	56
Joshua Thomas (8)	57
Matthew Percival (11)	57
Samantha Thomas (11)	58
Alex Rothe (10)	59
Casey Higgon	59
Christian Roberts (11)	60
Dafydd Phillips (11)	60

Llangwm VC Primary School, Haverfordwest

Amber White (10)	61
Eleanor Ewart (10)	61
Poppy Leggett (10)	62
Joseph Antonie Kiff (10)	62
Maddie Rees (11)	63
Charlote O'Donoghue (10)	63
James Griffiths (9)	64
Alice Edwards (9)	64

Llanybydder Primary School, Llanybydder

Jade Berry (10)	65
Ruth Davies (9)	65
Deloni Mair Davies (10)	66
Jordan James (10)	66
Ashley Bell (9)	67
Alice George (9)	67
Daniella Beaumont (10)	68
Emyr Wyn Jones (10)	69

Llechryd Primary School, Cardigan

Jack Cartwright (11)	69
Skye Heneker (10)	70
Samantha Francis (9)	70
Angharad Rees (11)	71
Olivia Stewart (11)	71
Hayley McLaughlin (11)	72
Amy Robinson (10)	72
Branwen Lewis (9)	73

Josie Westbury (10)	74
Steven Woodhouse (11)	74
Sarah Sommerville (10)	75
Hannah Sommerville (10)	75

Milford Haven Junior School, Milford Haven

Emma Groves (10) & Megan Williams (11)	76
Alice Brumby (11)	77
Rebecca Hearse Morgan & Lauren Owens (10)	78
Katie Edwards (10)	79
Elinor Roberts & Julie Potter (10)	80
Samantha Booth (11) & Jessica Thomas (10)	81
Jack Warby (10)	82
Niall Day & Andrew Smith (10)	83
Abby Wheeler & Jordan Reynolds (10)	84
Rhiannon Hobbs (10)	85
Sam Freeman (11)	86
Bradley James Cristofaro (9)	86
Libby Wheeler Smith (9)	87
Bethan Busby (9) & Emily Brock (10)	87
Alexandra Othen (10)	88
Jessica Whitby (9)	89
Sophie Williams (8)	89
Cathy Eaton (9)	90
Harley Nicholas (8)	91
Callum O'Donovan (8)	91
Naomi Wild (11)	92
Martyn White (10)	92
Dylan Larsen (9) & Ross Sutton (8)	93
Tamsin Mathias (8)	93
Jade Sims (10)	94
Gaynor Jeffries (10)	94
Rhiannon Mathias (10)	95
Alisha John (10)	95
Michael Hire (7)	96
Siôn Littlehales (11)	96
Abbie George (8)	97
Josh Kenniford (8)	97
Ben Davies (8)	98
Alex Carter (8)	98
Lauren Picton (7)	99

Verity White (11)	99
Cheyenne Butler (8)	100
Abby Wheeler & Rebecca Algieri (11)	100
Jonathan Craig (10)	101
Erin Smith (11)	101
Elizabeth Tamilia (10)	102
Lauren Littlehales (9)	103
Gabrielle Swales (9)	103
Hannah Jenkins (8)	104

Nant-Y-Groes Primary School, Ammanford

Emma While (11)	104
Shaun Williams (10)	105
Helen While (11)	105
Robert While (9)	106
Sioned Roberts (10)	106
Rachel Hall (10)	107

Ponthenri Primary School, Llanelli

Emyr Griffiths (10)	107
Nicholas Elms (10)	108
Scott Lewis (10)	108
Mickaela Regola (9)	109
Kayleigh Owen-Jones (11)	109
Leah Johnson (9)	110
Luke Emanuel (10)	110

Roch Community School, Haverfordwest

Nick Smith (8)	111
Steven Cristofaro (11)	111
Billy Brockbank (10)	112
Rhys Quigley (11)	112
Jessica Durham (10)	113
Andrew Ash (10)	113
Rebecca Mountstephens (9)	114
James Riddiford (10)	114
Abbie James (10)	115
Louis Hudson (10)	115
Bethan O'Shea (10)	116
Rhys Williams (9)	116

Ben Ford (9)	117
Alex Alderwick (11)	117
Laura Rogers, Katherine Smith & Rhian McConville (10)	118
Megan Jenkins (8)	118
Josh Watts (9)	119
James George (9)	119
Jodie Jones (9)	120
James Hughes (9)	120
Zoe Storrow (9)	121
Angharad Hughes (9)	121
Chloe Davies (10)	122
Charlotte Hughes (10)	122
Emil Matthews (9)	123

St Aidan's VA Primary School, Haverfordwest

Nia Lavis (9)	123
Alexandra Ridge (8)	124
George Jenkins (9)	124
Bethan Reynolds (9)	125
Laura Swain (9)	125
Jessica Viggars (9)	126
Emily Jones (9)	126
Morgana Dunwoody Kneafsey (9)	127
Laura Williams (8)	127
Katie Ridge (9)	128
Louise Wheatley (9)	128
Ashley Rees-Paton (9)	129
Iestyn Griffiths (9)	129
Ella Warner (9)	130
Megan Phillips (9)	130
Sophie Mills (9)	131
Rosanna Cale (9)	131
Heather Lewis (10)	132
Jordan Smith (9)	132
Gethin Williams (10)	133
Michael Dunwoody (9)	134
Daniel Casey (9)	134
Ruari Williams (8)	135
David Reynolds (8)	135
Josie Lewis (8)	135
Mollie Hughes (8)	136

Caitlin Thompson (7)   136
Lewis Evans (7)   136
Amy Rees (8)   137
Jessica Rees (7)   137
Louise Davies (8)   137
Tessa Page-Harries (8)   138
Rory Clague (8)   138
Ben Walton (8)   138
Katie Adams (7)   139
Liam Manwaring (8)   139
Sarah Bennett (8)   139
Josephine Maidment (11)   140
Abigail Severn (8)   140
Ben Clague (10) & Henry Partridge (11)   141
Jessica Lewis (10)   141
Stephanie Ridge (10)   142
Sophie Ellis (11)   142
Alice Bennett (10)   143
Michaela Protheroe (10)   143
Johnathon Stowell (9)   144
Thomas Evans (10)   144
William Squire (10)   145

St Mary's RC Primary School, Pembroke Dock
Jake Griffiths (7)   145
Rebecca Bradley (8)   146
Joseph McElroy (8)   146
Emma Wilson (7)   147
Christine Sassone (7)   147
Sophie Harris (9)   148
Joseph Harris (8)   149
Amy Brown (9)   149
Leanne Groves (9)   150
Ben Thomas (9)   150

St Oswald's VA School, Kilgetty
Laura Fursse (9)   150
Anna Lewis (11)   151
Matthew Lewis (10)   151
Richard Shaw (10)   152
Emily Tranter (10)   152

David Colquhoun (10)   153

Sageston CP School, Nr Tenby

Luke Hicks (10)   153
Jessica Clarke (10)   154
Beth Jackson (10)   154
Rebecca Mills (9)   155
Melissa Wilson (10)   155
Gareth Folder (9)   156
Wesley Hugh Bonser (10)   156
Rory Wynne-Owen (9)   157
Georgia Lewis (10)   157
Jessica Thomas (10)   158
Charlotte O'Rourke (10)   158
Rachael Robbins (9)   159
James Hinchliffe (9)   159
Oliver Cole (9)   160
Angharad Arnold (9)   160
Elle Joyce (10)   161
Robert Davenport (9)   162
Dominic Hicks (9)   162

Stepaside CP School, Kilgetty

George Coles (11)   163
Adam Beynon (11)   163
James Hughes (11)   164
Cai Harris (10)   165
Daniel Richards (11)   165
Kelsie Ormond (10)   166
Steven Brenchley (10)   166
James Griffiths (10)   167
Codie Jenkins (11)   168
Grace Bevan (10)   168
Lara Craig (10)   169
Owain Evans (10)   170
Rhys Bates (10)   171
Sam Page (11)   171
Stephen Harris (10)   172

Trecastle CP School, Brecon
Richie Elliott & Carwyn Pugh	172
Lowri Davies (9) & Caerwyn Davies (8)	173
Moses Hart & Jorden Davies (10)	173
Christabel Davies (10) & Sonny Annear (8)	173
Jamie Bourne (10)	174

Ysgol Carreg Hirfaen, Lampeter
Natalie Jones (9)	174
Melissa Carne (10)	175
Carwen Richards (9)	175
John Stacey Lewis (10)	176
Katy Jones (9)	176
Aled Williams (10)	177
Gethin Mathias (11)	177
Lynwen Mathias (9)	178
Delyth Mathias (8)	178
Kiri Douglas (7)	179
Lee Davies (7)	179
Lizzie Douglas (8)	180
Michaela Chalder (9)	180
Craig Richards (11)	181
Bethan Williams (10)	181
Rowan Marshall (9)	182
Tomos Williams (8)	182
Dylan Watkins (10)	183
Shaun Davies (8)	183
Christina Davies (10)	184
Sam Jacobs (9)	184
Rhys Price (9)	185
Cerys Roberts (9)	186
Sion Hughes (8)	186
Steffan Roberts (8)	187
Beca Creamer (8)	187
Dafydd Williams (9)	188
Dominic Lee (8)	188
Lloyd Richards (8)	188
Sioned Douglas (9)	189
Dylan Evans (8)	189
Lauren Gray (7)	190
Bethan Williams (7)	190

Nicola Jones (8)	190

Ysgol Griffith Jones, St Clears
Lowri David (9)	191
Wayne Broeckhoven (10)	191
Edward Noblett (9)	191
Brandon Davies (9)	192
Jodie Stickland (9)	192
Abbey Rees (9)	192
Amy Hill (10)	193
Lloyd Rees (9)	193
Ruth Elms	194
Flora Upton (9)	194

Ysgol Gynradd Cwmgors, Ammanford
Sarah Tomlinson (9)	195
Nicholas Jones (10)	195
Gemma Griffiths (10)	196
Jessica Jones (11)	196
Elin Angharad Halfpenny (10)	197
Lewis Reddy (10)	197
Andrew Smith (11)	198
Iestyn Jones (9)	199
Alex Horanszky (10)	200
Joseph O'Conner (10)	200
Joanna Elliott (11)	201
Megan Lewis (9)	201
Brittony Price (10)	202
Jade Johns (11)	203
Lucy Symons (11)	203
Rhys Williams (10)	204
Ben Cooke (10)	205

Ysgol Gynradd Wirfoddol Myfenydd, Llanrhystud
Richard Jones (10)	205
Jos Jones	206
Gwenllian Rees-Evans (10)	206
Aled Davies (10)	207
Eleanor Farley (10)	207
Edgar Bewers (9)	208

Sion Owen (9)	208
Gethin Davies (9)	209
Emma Morris (9)	209
Gareth Lloyd (11)	210
Joey Sinclair (10)	211
Ffion Tansley-Furr (9)	211
Marisa Morgan (9)	212
Ffion Evans (7)	212
Kathryn Botting (9)	213
Steffan Evans (11)	214
Jamie Tyler-Lloyd (8)	214
Andrew Fricker-Power (11)	215
Steffan Woodruff (11)	216
Michaela Richards (10)	217
Coral Kennerley (9)	217
Kara Knowler-Davies (11)	218
Sean François (8)	218
Rhys Nicholls (9)	219
Anwen Flynn (10)	219
Carys Evans (8)	220
Charlotte Robinson (9)	220
Louis Langford (8)	221
Heidi Hughes (8)	221
Alex Williams (7)	222
Catherine Nicole Richards (8)	222
Ioan Rees-Evans (8)	223

The Poems

Remembrance

The day they stopped to remember,
Was the day they'd never forget.
For they had been fighting,
In a war they'll always regret.

Guns here, cannons there,
Where do they get them all from?
Think of all the people who died,
And the families who knew they had gone.

So please will you think on this day,
This day which will always be here.
Think of all you have,
On this day of every year.

Lucy Webb (9)

Will You Play With Me?

Mum will you play with me?
You're always on the phone.
Mum will you play with me?
I'm feeling all alone.

Of course I will play with you
A little later on
When you have tidied your room
And the washing up is done.

Mum that's not fair
You always say that
Go and tidy this
And go and feed the cat.

You're in charge around here
You're my mum
I should go and play
Until 'your' work is done.

Well go and play then
And don't bother me
I'm coming to check your room
When I have had my cup of tea.

That's not fair, that's not fair
I did not make the mess
It's my little sister
She's the messy pest.

Just get up those stairs
Before I count to three.
That's not fair, that's not fair
You're always picking on me.

One, two . . . OK I'm going
I just wanted to play a game.
'Go and tidy your room'
It's always the flippin' same.

Mum where shall I put this?
What about my hat?
Will you put the books away
And vacuum the mat?

Just come down here
You're making my head a muddle
Open that cupboard door
And get a jigsaw puzzle.

But Mum I am busy
I am in the middle of a game
Could we do it later?
I don't mean to be a pain.

Lily May Usher (12)

The Scarlets

The Scarlets are the best team in the world,
Playing rugby and winning games, that's all they seem to do,
Against other teams from all over the world,
Their aim is to win the Heineken Cup,
Playing at home in Stradey Park,
What an honour that must be,
Playing the game must be so hard,
80 minutes of play in wet mud,
In rain and sun,
Any day of the week.
The Scarlets are the best team in the world.

Owen Rose (11)
Ciliau Parc Primary School, Lampeter

My Brother James

Jim Bob, Jamie, even James,
These are a few of my brother's names.
Cheeky, naughty sometimes nice,
Always playing with his knights.
Chasing the ball with our dad,
Football crazy, football mad.
Out of the bath, clean and cute,
All dressed up in his pyjama suit.
Time for bed, night-night James,
See you in the morning for more fun and games.

Rose Darlington (10)
Ciliau Parc Primary School, Lampeter

Dolphins

Dolphins are so wonderful,
My favourite animal in the world,
I wish I could own one,
All to myself.

Dolphins, dolphins they are great,
I love the noise they make,
Why can't I own one?
I'd care for it every day.

My mum said I wouldn't!
My dad said, 'You're too young!'
I say, 'It's not fair!'
But I know . . . eventually they'll give in!

Aimee Hughes (10)
Ciliau Parc Primary School, Lampeter

Fields

I really like fields
For in the spring
Everywhere I look
I see happy lambs playing.

The summer is nearly the same
For it is full of flowers, such as
Daisies, clover, buttercups,
Dandelions, cowslip and field scabious.

The autumn is alright,
The hedges start to die,
All the little flowers
Say goodbye.

When winter comes
The fields are beautifully
Covered from top to bottom in snow
And that is why I like fields.

Tom Wolfe (9)
Ciliau Parc Primary School, Lampeter

My Mum

My mum is the best,
She's better than the rest.
I'd give her a big kiss,
She is the greatest.

She is an angel in disguise,
She'd definitely win the 'best mum' prize.
She's always kind, good and true
And she'll say I love you.

Lauren Upshall (10)
Ciliau Parc Primary School, Lampeter

My School Dinners

Some people say they're awful,
But I say, *no way!*
They should come over one lunchtime
And try them, I say.

They're lovely and hot
As they bubble in the pot,
They are truly fantastic
Oh! I'm so ecstatic.

Finally, it's lunchtime
As we sit there in our seats,
Waiting with anticipation,
For lots of lovely treats.
Oh look, it's curry and rice -
My favourite food,
With cheesecake to follow,
I'm in a good mood.

To Edith the cook
What can I say?
But thank you so much
For our wonderful lunch each day.

Ruby Wakley (9)
Ciliau Parc Primary School, Lampeter

Rugby

Mud, mud, mud,
Fun, fun, fun,
As a game it's mean,
You never come home clean!

If your opponents play rough
You've got to be so tough!
If you miss the kick
They'll take the mick!

Charging, running, tackling,
Falling, playing, passing,
The other team's not your buddy,
Guaranteed you're very muddy.

I score a try,
Woweeeeeeeee!
Everyone runs
To congratulate me.

Morgan Davies (10)
Ciliau Parc Primary School, Lampeter

What Am I?

I jump out of the sea to see what I can see
I might be in a whale or shark family
I am bluey-grey and I eat prey.

People love me, some don't
But some people come and play with me
Mostly girls love me, but boys don't

What am I?
Dolphin.

Sarah Powell (10)
Crossgates Primary School, Llandrindod Wells

This Is A Tiger

This tiger . . .
Has eyes like sapphires burning in the moonlight
His eyes sparkle so much
You could see them from miles away.
That's his eyes.

He moves . . .
Swift like lightning, he's like a flash
He prowls while moving through the trees of rain
That's how he moves.

His voice . . .
Is like thunder shooting from a dark, gloomy sky
Any animal that hears his roar scarpers in an instant
That's his sound.

His fur glistens in the sun of midday like gems
And as soft as a teddy bear
That's fur.

Claws like razors, sharp and sparkle at all times
He's always ready to pounce on prey,
His claws.

His appearance ...
He stands tall and proud running through forests,
His claws grip the ground to run faster,
That's a tiger.

George Williams (10)
Crossgates Primary School, Llandrindod Wells

It Began

It began . . .
It snatches the softness of the clouds,
It snuck the whispiness of whipped cream,
For its mane.

It went on . . .
It took the sparkle of glitter
And the shine from the stars,
For its eyes.

It carried on . . .
It took the sharpness from the tip of the moon,
But borrowed the warmth from the sun
And made its paws.

It went on still . . .
It took the sleekness of a businessman's hair
And the silk from a sewer's room,
It had at last made its coat.

Then *it* became a lion.

Rhiannon Lewis (11)
Crossgates Primary School, Llandrindod Wells

Who Am I?

I have brown hair,
People say it's blonde.
I have gleaming brown eyes
Just like firing hazels in the sun.
I sometimes live in the zoo
And love to roll in poo!
I have a long furry mane
The colour of my chain.
Who am I?
Lion.

Andrea Burton (11)
Crossgates Primary School, Llandrindod Wells

Making A Lamb

She gathered the pinkness of candyfloss for her nose
She gathered the pearliness of pearls for her eyes
She gathered the curviness from a beach ball for her ears
And her face was made.

She gathered the fluffiness from the clouds in Heaven
She added the whiteness of Tipp-Ex to make the clouds even whiter
And her wool was made.

She gathered the screeching voices of a balloon to make her bleat
She gathered the personality and calmness from a mouse
She took the galloping of a horse
And the gentleness of a butterfly to make her walk
And lamb was made.

Annie Morris (11)
Crossgates Primary School, Llandrindod Wells

What Lion Stole

Lion stole the rasping sound,
That was as loud as a car
And made his voice.

For his coat and silky mane,
He took the colours of bronze and flame,
Also for his short, silver coat,
He added the softness of sandy coloured soap.

He moved like a blade through the long, lush grass,
Speeding, but silent,
As he ran like the wind.

Then at night his eyes lit up and he
Swiped sapphires for his dangerous, dancing eyes.

Fire and icicles described his claws best
And cat was made.

Rosie Stephens (11)
Crossgates Primary School, Llandrindod Wells

A Tiger Watching For Movement In The Air

His eyes sparkled like huge white
Stars in the vast sky watching
For movement in the air.

He prowled slowly through the
Mist like a slug in the bright sun
Watching for movement in the
Air.

His voice whispered slowly
So that he could hear
Something coming like
Prey coming towards
Him watching for
Movement in the air.

He felt soft and warming to my touch
And his ghostly fur felt short and
Delicate watching for movement
In the air.

His claws, sharp as a razor can
Be heard clicking, waiting for
Something to come, watching
For movement in the air.

If you see this animal you
Will see him in a ghostly form,
Watching for movement in the air.

Matthew Jones (11)
Crossgates Primary School, Llandrindod Wells

Mr Rabbit

Mr Rabbit ran
Mr Rabbit swiped the sunset for his lovely soft voice.

Mr Rabbit swiped a diamond from the queen's crown
For his lovely white coat
And swiped some coal and stars for his black, sparkly eyes.

Mr Rabbit swiped the movement from a shark
So he could whizz around.

Then at night
Mr Rabbit grabbed the stars for his lovely sparkly eyes.

Mr Rabbit's claws are from a tiger
Because they are sharp like their teeth.

Rabbit is home.

Emma Collins (10)
Crossgates Primary School, Llandrindod Wells

Tiger

Tiger started
Tiger took the leaves of the trees
And the darkness of the night to make his eyes.

Tiger took the roar of the bear,
He took the dragon's talons to make his claws.

Tiger took the strength of the dragon to make his strength.

Tiger took the noise from the trees,
He took the whistling of the wind to make his voice.

Tiger took the running of the cheetah
And the walk of the zebra to make his movement.

Tiger took the colour of the sun for his coat,
He took the laugh of a hyena.

Tiger was born.

Gary Pritchard (11)
Crossgates Primary School, Llandrindod Wells

Making A Koala

Making a koala
She gathered the dark sky,
She gathered the shine of the stars
And made her eyes.

For her ears,
She gathered the point from a needle,
She gathered the shape of a pyramid,
She gathered the wideness of the ocean.

From the seaside,
She gathered the movement from the waves,
She gathered the slender movement of a bird, for her walk.

For her claws,
She gathered the sharpness of broken glass,
She gathered the hardness of a rock, to grab on to the trees.

Making a koala,
She gathered the softness of cotton wool
And for her figure she gathered the roundness of a plum.

And there you have - your koala bear.

Kashika Paris (10)
Crossgates Primary School, Llandrindod Wells

Crow Began

Crow began
He took the black of the night for his feathers,
He took the black of the coal for his eyes.

He took the scales of a snake for his legs,
He took the fingers of the Devil for his claws,
He took the speed of the leopard.

He scraped the mind of a bat,
He took a spear for his beak
And crow was made.

Nathan Dunn (10)
Crossgates Primary School, Llandrindod Wells

To Create A Dragon

To create a dragon
You must acquire the ancient fire
You must acquire the volcanic lava
To make his breath.

For his dark, evil eyes
You must acquire blood-red rubies
You must acquire the shadows of the night.

To make his scales
You must acquire chain-mail from the Himalayas
You must acquire the metals of the spirit world.

And for the scales
You must acquire the strongest materials from all over the galaxy
You must acquire the steels from the volcanic rock.

To create dragon,
You acquire the fear of young men who have fallen before him,
You must acquire the anger and hatred of those who feel hate
To make his mind.

And dragon was born!

Curtis Leavesley (11)
Crossgates Primary School, Llandrindod Wells

My Sleeping Problem

At night I just can't sleep,
I think too much and fall too deep,
I cannot find the land of nod
And the sandman is not doing his job.

One night of sleep that's all I need,
So man in the moon do a good deed.
So one night just, just let me sleep,
Before my problem gets too deep.

Evie Doman (11)
Crossgates Primary School, Llandrindod Wells

At The Pool

A smell of chlorine fills the air,
Lifeguard watching from his chair.

Flume and rapids are exciting,
Bubbling jacuzzi looks inviting.

There are gentle shallows which babies need,
A twenty-five metre pool, great for speed.

Shouts, laughter and splashing sounds all mingle,
Water in my eyes makes them tingle.

I smile when I see the *No Diving* sign,
Mrs Jones lets us when it's lesson time!

The showers feel too hot after being in the pool,
I'll buy an ice cream at reception then I'll soon be cool.

Gareth Morgan (11)
Forden CW Primary School, Welshpool

A Magical Dream

A magical dream with fairies and elves -
With lots of potions on their shelves.

A magical dream with witches and spells -
And old mysterious wishing wells.

A magical dream with wizards and knights -
And wonderful, compelling warlock fights.

A magical dream with a moonlit pond -
A mermaid singing an enchanting song.

That's my magical dream!

Megan Dyer (10)
Forden CW Primary School, Welshpool

The Night Magician

Thickly dark like drawn velvet curtains until he comes.
Fearful, like the insecurity of blindness until he comes.
Silent, like the deafness of the grave until he comes -
He turns darkness into light - when he comes
He turns fear into security - when he comes
He turns silence into a silent comfort - when he comes
The moon . . . The Night Magician.

Fabian Twist (11)
Forden CW Primary School, Welshpool

The Magic Box
(Based on 'Magic Box' by Kit Wright)

I will put in the box . . .
the sounds of my favourite songs,
the clapping of the cheering crowds,
the splashing of the water around me.

I will put in the box . . .
the love of a hug from my nan,
the laughter that follows a silly joke.

I will put in the box . . .
the crunch of the leaves under my feet,
the noise of the rain on the roof,
the howl of the wind.

I will put in the box . . .
the rustling of Christmas paper,
the smell of Christmas spices,
the smiles on my family's faces.

My box is built from dark, black wood
covered with bright, shiny leather,
with golden studs on the top.

I shall swim in my box
in front of the world,
in the Olympic stadium.

Alex Charlesworth (9)
Guilsfield CP School, Welshpool

My Mum

My mum is an 'It's up to you.'
Kind of mum.
A 'Come on you have to decide now or you're not going'
Kind of mum.
A sort of 'No chocolate today, only Fridays, Saturdays and Sundays'
Kind of mum.

A sort of 'We're going now'
'Hurry up, it's time for school'
Kind of mum.

An 'I'm leaving without you'
'I'm busy, we'll do it later,' kind of mum.

She is the kind of lady that says, 'What do you want for breakfast? But you have to have something else because there are no chocolate croissants left.'

She is champion of . . .
Working in the school,
Organising everybody
And helping other people.
She is the sort of mum that loves animals.

But most of all she is someone who is always there for me.

Danielle Pearce (8)
Guilsfield CP School, Welshpool

The Magic Box
(Based on 'Magic Box' by Kit Wright)

I will put in my box . . .
The soft, silky feel of a silvery dressing gown,
The head of a huge fire-breathing dragon, Smaug,
The enormous baggy mane of a lion, brushing against my face.

I will put in my box . . .
The foggy moor, next to Baskerville Hall,
A leaf from the tallest redwood tree, standing high in the forest,
The hoof of an antelope, charging over the plains of Africa.

I will put in my box . . .
The sword of an Arabian king, lost forever,
The last sigh of a grandad, gone to a better place
And the first word of a baby, treasured by its mother forever.

I will put in my box . . .
A pitch-black tiger, hunting in the moonlight
And a stripy panther, climbing a dead tree,
A 5cm tall house, which nobody lives in.

My box is crafted from . . .
Oak, beech and evergreen wood,
With elfish carvings on the lid and sides,
Its hinges are vines grown on the thickest tree
                            of the Amazon rain forest.

I will glide on my box . . .
Over the Atlantic ocean
Over the horizon
And never return.

Henry Richards (10)
Guilsfield CP School, Welshpool

Magic Box
(Based on 'Magic Box' by Kit Wright)

I will put in my box . . .
A beautiful bandanna, beaded and shining
A magical unicorn horn, special in every way
My fingertips stroking a fur rug.

I will put in my box . . .
A bendy sun ray reaching out
A single petal from a foreign rose
And exotic colours from a tropical fish.

I will put in my box . . .
A secret spoken in Spanish
The last smile of a long-lost friend
And the first steps of a toddler.

I will put in my box . . .
A pink caterpillar and a water-worried fish
A height-frightened monkey
And a red moonbeam.

My box is crafted from woven grass
And the juice of a strawberry to colour it
It's speckled with emeralds and rubies.

I will fly on my box . . .
To the red moon and beyond
And gently fall asleep
With all my memories in my box.

Bethany Dodd (10)
Guilsfield CP School, Welshpool

Magic Box
(Based on 'Magic Box' by Kit Wright)

I will put in the box . . .
A fluffy sheep's woollen coat shining with pearls
A ginger hair from the head of a mermaid
And the feel of the autumn tree trunk.

I will put in the box . . .
The lovely warm heat from the sun
A precious rock from the tip of Gros Biton
A feather from a golden eagle.

I will put in the box . . .
A sizzle of summer in a floating heat haze
The last whisper from a caring soul
And the first cry from a newborn baby.

My box is created from . . .
Gold and silver swirls carved into it
The texture is almost like sandpaper, rough and rugged.

I will go on adventures in my box
To places far and wide
And lose myself in a dream.

Abbie Knight (10)
Guilsfield CP School, Welshpool

Tanks Drove Through The Mud Haiku

Tanks drove through the mud
Tracks are struck, sinking, drowning
Lots of lives lost here.

Rhys Jones (11)
Guilsfield CP School, Welshpool

The Magic Box
(Based on 'Magic Box' by Kit Wright)

I will put in the box . . .
The sway of a silver, shining skirt
Black dribble from a three-headed dog
The feel of a coarse and wrinkled elephant skin.

I will put in the box . . .
A flash of lightning, glowing in the midnight sky
A pure drop from the largest waterfall
The speed of a single cheetah.

I will put in the box . . .
A magic, glistening, glossy bubble
The last smile of my beloved uncle
And the first sneeze of a delightful cousin.

I will put in the box . . .
A dog with a purr
And a cat with a woof
A white sun and a yellow moon.

My box is created from . . .
Oak wood shining in the sun
With hinges of gold, carved
And locks of burnished bronze.

I shall escape in my box . . .
Into a never, never land
And stay there forever.

Katie Davies (10)
Guilsfield CP School, Welshpool

The Magic Box
(Based on 'Magic Box' by Kit Wright)

I will put in the box . . .
A swish of a swaying silver skirt
An ivory tooth from the jaw of a woolly mammoth
The softness of fur worn by a silky white cat.

I will put in the box . . .
A rainbow arc glowing in the sun
The sight of a golden mirage
A phenomenally fast footstep of a giant jaguar.

I will put in the box . . .
A genie from a bottle blue
The last blink of an elderly man
And the first step of a toddler.

I will put in my box . . .
A dog with a shell
And a snail with a kennel
Black snow and white ink.

My box is fashioned from gold, silver and bronze
With every jewel imaginable in each corner
And secret scale hinges.

I shall explore in my box
Among the crafted jewels
In a sea of animals
And through the rainbow's pot of gold.

Jessica Thomas (10)
Guilsfield CP School, Welshpool

The Magic Box
(Based on 'Magic Box' by Kit Wright)

I will put in the box . . .
My woolly hat and gloves from a ram's rugged body
Eye of Cyclops staring into the east.
A touch of steel from a jaguar racing at 80mph in the desert.

I will put in the box . . .
A drop of rain the colour of turquoise, feeding the Atlantic ocean
A stone from my mystery waterfall, just for me
The spark of an angelfish directing it in its underworld depths.

I will put in the box . . .
Three shooting stars from my dream - my only friends
The last meal with Jesus Christ
And the first baby, called Dylan.

I will put in the box . . .
Thirteen months
A nun on a broom, a vicar on a horse
A person with two left feet.

My box is modelled from gossamer webs
With hinges of crocodile skin
And a lock of tiger tooth.

I will ski on my box
Over Antarctic avalanches
In blizzard and storm
Then return home to warmth and cocoa.

Gwynnfore Evans (11)
Guilsfield CP School, Welshpool

What's That In My Room?

Argh, what's that?
It's a mouse.
No, it's the door
It's creaking.
Argh, what's that?
It's thumping
No, it's the dogs.
Argh, what's that?
It's loud owls twitting.
Argh, what's that?
It's purring
It's just a cat.
Argh, what's that?
It's petrifying.
Argh, what's that?
I'm shivering
I'm still scared.

Argh, what's that?

Ellen Banner (8)
Haverfordwest VC School, Haverfordwest

Darkness

I was in my bed
It was scary
The door was creaking
I heard the door opening
I heard footsteps
It was my mum.

Jacob Thomas (8)
Haverfordwest VC School, Haverfordwest

What's That In The House?

Everyone was in their beds
I was still awake
I was scared
I could hear something outside my bedroom door
I heard footsteps
Clip, clop, clip, clop
I heard my mum and dad whispering
I was imagining ghosts in my closet
I heard the wind howling
My blood went cold
It was spooky
Argh! It's a ghost
Argh! I'm scared
My heart is thumping
Mum and Dad are still whispering
Echoing through the wall
Finally I realised it's not a ghost.

Elin Newton (8)
Haverfordwest VC School, Haverfordwest

Night

One night when I went upstairs
Suddenly it was complete darkness
I turned and it was *creepy*
I heard a . . . *creak!*
Spread across the room
Another sound came
It made the sound tu-whit tu-whoo!
Tu-whit tu-whoo!
I was terrified
A big shadow went up the wall
I turned
It was my dad
What are you doing out of bed?

Thomas Easton (8)
Haverfordwest VC School, Haverfordwest

The Horrible Dark Night

Lying in bed I can see shadows
I am terrified
I start chattering my teeth
I start calling my mum
She can't hear me
I start crying
I can hear my door creaking slowly
I try and get myself down
But I can't
I can hear the wind
Is it a ghost?
I don't know
I am scared
I can hear pipes clinking and clanging
The springs in my bed
I hear my mum and dad watching telly
I hear an owl
I can see a lamp outside my window flickering
My door starts banging
My cat comes in and starts licking my face
I can hear something falling over
But it was next door's dog tipping something over
Lying in bed I can see shadows.

Danielle Thomas (8)
Haverfordwest VC School, Haverfordwest

Night-Time

When I went to bed
I heard the door creak
I was scared
I thought there was a ghost
I went under the quilt.

Joshua Ward (8)
Haverfordwest VC School, Haverfordwest

Scare Me

In the darkness
A door creaks and bangs
I hear the pipes creaking
I can hear my mum and dad watching television.
The wind is going *whoo* or is it a ghost?
I am really scared!
I can hear an owl hooting outside.
Through my bedroom window I can see a street lamp flickering
I hear a crash!
But it is only next-door's dog knocking something over.
A cat is miaowing for its tea.
I am terrified!
My sister is scared of the dark
She is crying.
Mummy is coming up the stairs
Or is it a bogey man?
A baby is screaming next door
My blood runs cold
The moon is shining like a circle of light
That the sun has sent up.

Kirsty Lewis (7)
Haverfordwest VC School, Haverfordwest

Bedtime

It was Friday night
I was in bed
It was dark
In a shadow I saw a shark
I was scared
Then I heard a *whoosh!*
It was only the wind.
It blew down something that was pinned to my wall
My eyes start closing
My eyelids are getting heavy
I'm drifting off to sleep.

Luke Eden (8)
Haverfordwest VC School, Haverfordwest

Darkness Has Arrived

I was in my bed,
My door was creaking open.
I was in my bed, I saw a shadow
Come up on my wall.
I was in my bed,
The darkness was arriving.
I was in my bed,
I heard some footsteps coming up my stairs.
My heart was pounding and fluttering,
It was really *creepy*.

Jessica James (7)
Haverfordwest VC School, Haverfordwest

Night

One night when I was going to bed
There was a flash of lightning
It became complete darkness
My heart was banging, tu-whit tu-whoo
I ran into my bedroom
I was chattering my teeth
There was a glow
I was petrified
Boom - a car door
'Mum, Mum.'
'Shh! We're watching the football.'

Richard Thomas (7)
Haverfordwest VC School, Haverfordwest

School Days

School days, boys and girls jump about.
School days, they love to shout.
School days, boys play football.
School days, girls play tag.
School days, they love to slide.
School days, they spin about.
School days, they have sport days.
School days, until the school holidays.
School days, until it's home time.

Alex Roberts (8)
Haverfordwest VC School, Haverfordwest

The Night Before Hallowe'en

It was the night before Hallowe'en
I didn't know what to dream
I was too frightened to dream
So I let out a scream, 'Argh!'
I shivered in my dream
I woke up and screamed
Phew it was only a dream.

Lucy Campbell (7)
Haverfordwest VC School, Haverfordwest

Dear Snow

I wish you would come to Haverfordwest
Then we can jump in the snow.
I wish you would come to Haverfordwest
Then we can fall in the snowdrift.
I wish you would come to Haverfordwest
Then we can watch the snowflakes drop.
I wish you would come to Haverfordwest
Then we can watch the snow fall from the sky.
I wish I could wake up and find my garden white.

Tommy-Lee Vores (8)
Haverfordwest VC School, Haverfordwest

The Magic Web

Scuttling and scurrying across its web
Tripping over each and every thread.
The web is jewelled from the rain
Icicles hanging from the windowpane.
Making sure every thread is in its own silk circle
The spider wonders when her web will complete another world
The silk smooth has surrounded a window with its magnificent web
Snowflakes fall on the frosty web.
Soon enough you make out the snowy city.
It's a place filled with hopes and dreams
Towers start to appear from the web
Children waving, others playing, people singing
As pale as snow their hair compares to the icy frost
Snowflakes falling, children calling from the magic web.

Jessica Davies (10)
Haverfordwest VC School, Haverfordwest

Snow

Snow is glittery and shiny
Snow, it's very pretty, it shines like angels' wings
Snow, it sparkles like glitter on your top
Icicles are really fragile
Snow, it gleams like glass
Snow, it's really sparkly
Snow, it's really beautiful
Snow is the nicest weather
Snow makes me happy.

Bethan Hoare (8)
Haverfordwest VC School, Haverfordwest

Dear Rain

Dear Rain,
Please come and make big puddles
Maybe even a new pond
I would be out for hours and hours
And if you turn into a storm
I would be allowed to have some nice, warm hot chocolate.

Please turn into a snowstorm.
Please turn out the lights
Then there will be total darkness all night
With lightning coming again and again and *again*!
My dog will be scared *until* the storm is over
Please come,
Love from Carli.

Carli Absalom (8)
Haverfordwest VC School, Haverfordwest

Jack Frost

Jack Frost is sparkling
You will see him in the night.
Snow is coming down
It will land on the rooftop.
It will shine on the ground
And it will be fluttering down.
Snow is fun, it is happy and exciting
Robins sing in the tree
Rabbits are in their homes
Squirrels are looking for nuts.

Emily Pemberthy (8)
Haverfordwest VC School, Haverfordwest

A Cold Winter's Night

One cold night
It was breezy, freezy, noisy
The lights went out
Darkness!
Out of the darkness came snow.
Little specks of ice falling through the sky.
It was like one hundred falling stars
Falling softly, softly, softly.
A freezy world everywhere.

Jacob Arnold (8)
Haverfordwest VC School, Haverfordwest

Jack Frost

Look out, look out!
Jack Frost is about!
He's coming to bite our fingers.
Look out! Look out!
Jack Frost is about!
He will give you *frostbite!*
Look out! Look out!
Jack Frost is about!
Oh look, it's snowing now
It's snowing.

Joe Lloyd (9)
Haverfordwest VC School, Haverfordwest

Snow

Snow is freezy, breezy.
Snow is twinkling, slippy
Snow is like snowflakes falling on ice.
Snow is like twinkling snowflakes.
Snow is melting.
Snow is freezy and gleamy.
Snow is cold and freezy on trees
Snow is bitter like ice.
Snow is wonderful.
Snow falls in winter and makes us happy.

Leanne John (8)
Haverfordwest VC School, Haverfordwest

The Ice

It is freezy
It is joyful
It's a surprise.
It is skiddy
It is glittering
It glows.
It is dangerous
It is silvery
It's freezing cold
It is slippery
It is icy.

Louise Morris (8)
Haverfordwest VC School, Haverfordwest

Monsters

Monsters are evil,
They will go to a planet,
Fight its inhabitants
And send them away forever.

They have many heads and lots of eyeballs,
They really like to kill.

So we're going to fight them
And defeat them
And banish them from the universe
And if they come back we'll kill them all.

Lucas Horton (8)
Haverfordwest VC School, Haverfordwest

Snow

Snow is very cold.
It is freezy, breezy.
Ice is slippery
Ice is fun.
But . . .
Do not slip, you will fall.
But do snow
Just for me.
I wish you over me.
Please snow!

Roxanne Griffiths (8)
Haverfordwest VC School, Haverfordwest

Snow

The snowflakes fall from the grey sky
While the ice mountain cracks in half,
The city freezes to death when the
White frost covers it.
The lake is frozen to the spot,
Covered with spotless ice.
The ice, the snow and the frost all remind
Us of the great Ice Age, with its
Odd and scary creatures.
I just wish that it would come back next year.

Rhys Morris (8)
Haverfordwest VC School, Haverfordwest

Snow

Snowmen
Snow cones
Snowballs
Snow boots
Freezing
Snow
Watery
White
Freezy
Crunchy
Squishy
Ice Age.

Ryan Wilson (9)
Haverfordwest VC School, Haverfordwest

Storm

A bird fighter
A roof taker
A door banger
A branch cracker
A strong blower
An animal scarer
A sea crasher
A tree smasher.

Ryan Scott & Rhys Thomas (8)
Haverfordwest VC School, Haverfordwest

Night

An owl waker,
A leaf shaker,
A sleep maker,
A dream catcher,
A bed cosier,
A star brighter,
A sun fighter,
A moon lighter.

Connor Nurse (8)
Haverfordwest VC School, Haverfordwest

Dear Snow

Dear Snow,
Please come to my winter party.
I hope you don't melt on your way.
You have to come quickly
Otherwise it will be morning again
So please, please come.
From Tommy.

Tommy Bolstridge Edwards (8)
Haverfordwest VC School, Haverfordwest

Christmas Haiku

Lights around the fire
Decorations on the tree
Stars along the path.

Sophie Russell (10)
Hendy-Gwyn Primary School, Whitland

Seasons Haiku

Birds are flying south
Fields are so very cold now
Animals are in.

Eilesha Clarke (10)
Hendy-Gwyn Primary School, Whitland

Seasons

In spring the plants grow,
In summer go to the beach,
In autumn leaves fall.

Lucy Duncombe (11)
Hendy-Gwyn Primary School, Whitland

Seasons Haiku

Damp weather is cold
The rain gets you very wet.
You get very wet.

Ella Storer (10)
Hendy-Gwyn Primary School, Whitland

June Haiku

My birthday in June
I love it because it's hot
And we play outside.

Jasmine Sterndale (10)
Hendy-Gwyn Primary School, Whitland

Seasons Haiku

The plants are dying
it is becoming winter
And that means no sun.

Josef Watson (9)
Hendy-Gwyn Primary School, Whitland

Seasons Haiku

Plants are coming now,
Daffodils are coming up
Animals have young.

Nikita Evans (10)
Hendy-Gwyn Primary School, Whitland

Classroom Haiku

In the big classroom
Children are turning pages
And doing their work.

Daniel Chick (10)
Hendy-Gwyn Primary School, Whitland

Christmas Is . . .

Christmas is singing carols, pulling crackers,
Eating satsumas and raising glasses.

Building snowmen, writing cards,
Feeding robins in the yard.

Celebrating, having fun,
Eating mince pies, one by one.

Looking for Rudolph and his sleigh,
Hoping that Santa is on his way.

Opening presents, large and small,
Hanging tinsel on the wall.

Church bells ringing loud and clear,
Hush is that Santa's sleigh I hear?

Remembering baby Jesus, when He was born,
This is why we celebrate, every Christmas morn.

Kyle Naylor (11)
Hendy-Gwyn Primary School, Whitland

Seasons Haiku

Special things happen
The sheep have their sweet small lambs
Spring is back again.

Sophie Jackson (11)
Hendy-Gwyn Primary School, Whitland

Cawl

Cawl, cawl is the king of all soups,
It feels like a free-flowing piece of chewing gum
Running down your throat.

It smells like a bottle of perfume,
It tastes fragrant and savoury.

Try it with the best organic Welsh vegetables,
Fine beef, try it with cheese and a slice of bread.
Most importantly of all, remember the leek!

No matter how you try it
You'll always be back for more
Atmospheric character, a true taste of home.

Cawl smells so nice, you can follow it in the air
A pot of yellow, green and white, replenishing vegetables
It's gold dust!
Eat it quickly or it will soon disappear.

Nothing beats cawl!

Daniel Benjamin (10)
Lakefield Primary School, Llanelli

The Magnificent Kitten

My magnificent kitten Ben.
My Ben is brown and grey, like a fly,
His cry is like a child's crying in pain.
His fur is like a soft blanket on a bed,
His eyes are like twinkling stars in the midnight sky.
He resembles a hedgehog hibernating in the winter,
I will love him and care for him
Forever!
My Ben.

Shaldon Hayes (9)
Lakefield Primary School, Llanelli

Cawl

Smell the beautiful cawl,
Cooking on the old iron cauldrons
In Llanelli.
It's March the first
You can feel it in the air.
Welsh singing, traditional music
And the best dish of them all.
Oh, I do like cawl!
Mum, please can you make me some cawl!

The finest blend of vegetables and sweetmeat,
Cawl is the taste of spring, an explosion of culture.

I eat it slowly with a wooden spoon and bowl
and a slice of Caerphilly cheese.

Mum, please cook me some cawl!

Ben Davies (10)
Lakefield Primary School, Llanelli

My Cawl Poem

Cawl, cawl is first class,
Lovely and lumpy, make it last.
March the first, I'm so excited,
To taste the flavour, ready and waiting.
You might think it's ordinary soup,
But I think it's rather special,
Flavoursome stock,
Perfumed vegetables.
A cauldron full of spice and life.

Lewis Williams (10)
Lakefield Primary School, Llanelli

My Little Sister

My little sister to me is a brat,
Just like next-door's black and white cat,
But she isn't terribly fat,
Just flat.

My little sister is quiet in school,
But when she comes home I feel like drowning in a pool
And although I take her for a fool,
I've heard she's quite clever.

My little sister, clever?
Never!
When she comes home she's always been falling for my jokes
And will be, forever.

My little sister is a lot of worry
And that's why I want to leave in such a hurry,
Go to McDonald's and buy a McFlurry,
With a nice hot spicy curry!

Jake Rees (11)
Lakefield Primary School, Llanelli

The Moon

The moon shines . . .
Like a polished mirror in the night sky
Floats like a silver balloon in a disco hall
Glows like a candle flame, lighting up our hearts
Smiles like a smiling clown in a circus
Sparkles like glitter on a Christmas card
Spins like a pebble in the water.

Carly McCann (10)
Lakefield Primary School, Llanelli

Mother Nature

The blazing sun - the finest power.
Raindrops twinkle by the hour.
The crackling leaves,
The stars a-shine,
The seashore swishes along the line.
As the moon says goodbye
The sun rises high in the sky.

Glistening frost on the ground,
Underfoot makes quite a sound.
So Mother Nature says goodbye,
A good night's rest for the people
But wait, a colourful rainbow with
Orange, yellow, red and green -
The prettiest colours I have seen.

Adam Entwistle (10)
Lakefield Primary School, Llanelli

The Magnificent Max

The magnificent fish
My fish is silver and gold
Like the reflection of the moon on moonlit waters
His fins are like rainbows across the sky
His body is like the crescent moon
His eyes are like little ping-pong balls
He resembles a crystal in a bowl of colour
I will feed him and clean his bowl
Max.

Ainsley Brown (9)
Lakefield Primary School, Llanelli

Alanna

Alanna
Playful, active, energetic and happy
Daughter of Valerie and David
Lover of chips, chocolate and sausages
Who feels bored at home and joyful in school
Who finds happiness in my parents
Who needs love all the time
Who gives my rabbit a bath, now and again
Who fears wasps and dragonflies
Who would like to see Florida
Who enjoys dancing and hip hop music
Who likes wearing black trousers
Resident of Llanelli
James.

Alanna James (10)
Lakefield Primary School, Llanelli

The Magnificent Dog

The magnificent dog,
My dog Scampy is yellow and enthusiastic
Like a lively, bouncy ball.
His magnificent eyes are like glowing stars
In the dark night sky.
His huge ears are like the wings of flapping birds,
His nose is like a big pink marshmallow.
He resembles a glowing fire,
I will look after him and
Take him for walks,
I'll protect him.
Scampy.

Chloe Thomas (10)
Lakefield Primary School, Llanelli

Cawl

Crunchy carrots boiling all day
Take my breath away.
Amazing lamb, mouth-watering
With a hot bun and cheese.
Whistling soup with a super smell
Heavenly and delicious.
Lovely leeks with a hint of salt,
It's a Welsh thing - Cawl!

Bethany Nicholas (9)
Lakefield Primary School, Llanelli

The Dragon

A dragon is fierce,
A dragon is mean
But this dragon is the nicest I've seen.
With his great red body
And very long tail.
If you see him you'll
Soon run away.

Jessica Colwill (10)
Lakefield Primary School, Llanelli

Cawl

Take the meat put it in a bowl,
add some vegetables
and they're ready to go.

Carrots, parsnips, onions,
potatoes, leeks and swede.
I can't wait to eat it,
this is just what I need.

Lovely, tasty cawl!

Alex Mears (10)
Lakefield Primary School, Llanelli

Sophie

Sophie
Short, happy, playful and active
Daughter of Jonathan and Luci
Lover of chips, biscuits and animals
Who feels energetic on Saturday and bored on Sundays
Who finds happiness in friends and brother
Who needs hugs now and again
Who gives the cat a bath
Who fears spiders and flies
Who would like to see Alaska
Who enjoys swimming and pop music
Who likes to wear black cords and white tops
Resident of Llanelli
Hope.

Sophie Hope (10)
Lakefield Primary School, Llanelli

The Stuff In Autumn

Leaves start falling off the trees
All you hear is the crackle from the leaves.
All night long the leaves start to fall
Curling and twirling through the storm
The animals go to hibernate when the squirrel
Gathers its nuts
Who will be first down the tree?

Georgia Shephard (8)
Lakefield Primary School, Llanelli

Birthdays

Birthdays are lots of fun,
Lots of fun for everyone.
Party poppers swirling down,
Seeing balloons all around.

Here comes the birthday cake
It smells lovely, it's home-made.
The candles are shining bright,
Reflected by the window light.

It's time for the children to go home,
They don't want to go, they decide to *moan!*

Lucy Green (9)
Lakefield Primary School, Llanelli

The Pussy Cat

Pussy cat, pussy cat,
Where are you?
Are you in the attic
Or are you under the stairs?
Are you in the bathroom?
Are you in the kitchen?
He might even be in my bedroom
Sleeping on my clothes!
He could be in the washing basket
But he wouldn't like it there.
Pussy cat, he's been sleeping in the greenhouse.

Andreas Taffetsauffer (8)
Lakefield Primary School, Llanelli

The Cat

Once there was a cat
Big and black,
Nice and fat.
He was good,
He was nice,
He was in a mood.
He was in front of the fire,
He was in front of the chair,
What did he desire?
He was friendly,
He was kind,
He wanted to meet the world.

He had a basket,
He had a bowl,
He liked resting.
He had a home,
He likes his house,
He likes his dome.
He has friends,
He has brothers,
He has a family.

He has owners,
He has food,
He loves his owners.
His sisters are kind,
His brothers are kind,
He is kind.

Ashley Copeman (9)
Lakefield Primary School, Llanelli

My Poem

I smashed a glass in my class,
It landed on the floor,
Then someone knocked the door.
When I went there she said, 'Take care!'
It was time for dinner.
I had fish and peas
And then I banged my knee.
I told the teacher, she said, 'Oh dear!'
Home time is coming near.

Annelise Davies (9)
Lakefield Primary School, Llanelli

Cawl

You have to put cawl in a pot
Make it very nice and hot,
But if you add lots of spice
You will find it not very nice.
Carrots and parsnips and leeks
Are better for you than loads of sweets.

Heather Hurt (8)
Lakefield Primary School, Llanelli

My Best Friend

My best friend is nice and kind
She is very smart and speaks her mind
She's all the friend that I could have
And her name is Lucy Green.

Gemma Williams (9)
Lakefield Primary School, Llanelli

Charlotte

C harming, smiley, always happy
H elpful, caring
A lways chatting
R osy cheeks and fiery hair
L oves to be trendy and wear clothes with a flair
O nly nine, but acts much older
T winkly eyes that smile for her
T otally a joy
E veryone adores her.

Charlotte Morrison (9)
Lakefield Primary School, Llanelli

Cawl

When the rain is falling
And the wind begins to howl,
Nothing warms your belly,
Like a healthy bowl of cawl.
With fresh winter vegetables
And tasty tender meat,
Celebrating St David's Day,
Becomes a special treat.

Jessica Withers (8)
Lakefield Primary School, Llanelli

Spring

S ometimes it rains, sometimes it shines
P retty leaves are growing fast
R ainbow flowers appear at last
I n the trees, birds are singing
N earby, bells are ringing
G rass is sparkling.

Carys James (9)
Lakefield Primary School, Llanelli

March The First

March the first, Saint David's Day
Very hungry, we all say
Fancy something hot to eat?
A bowl of this goes down a treat?

Carrot, onion, leek and swede
Gives the goodness that we need
Fill the saucepan to the top
Stir it up and make it hot

Set the table, all sit down
Taste the best food in town
Add some pepper if you wish
Get ready for this tasty dish

Cawl is lovely food to eat
Full of chunks of juicy meat
Some like it with a lump of cheese
Serve us up a bowl, oh please!

Liam Green (7)
Lakefield Primary School, Llanelli

Autumn Leaves

Autumn leaves all fall down
Squirrels come out to play
All the leaves start to dry
Autumn apples all fall down
All the leaves go out to fly
Until autumn goes by
And all the leaves say goodbye.

Siân Jones-Higginson (8)
Lakefield Primary School, Llanelli

Cawl

Cawl is a soup
Delicious soup too
You eat it in the winter
And it warms you right through
My mum puts lovely lamb in
Potatoes and vegetables too
When it's cooked altogether
It's very healthy and tastes good too
So when you're feeling hungry
And you don't know what to do
Ask your mum to try it
You'll be glad you tried it too.

Rubell Khan (8)
Lakefield Primary School, Llanelli

Cawl

Cawl is warm
On a winter's night.
Steaming hot
In a big round pot
Carrots, potatoes, onions, leeks,
Parsley and lamb
It's such a treat.
Mammy makes it all through the year
But wintertime is best,
We have a big bowl
And then another,
Then Mammy says,' Who wants the rest?'
In school on March first
It is St David's Day,
We celebrate by eating cawl
Then we go out to play.

Jordan Howe (8)
Lakefield Primary School, Llanelli

Cawl! Cawl! Cawl!

Chop! Chop! Chop! Mum is slicing leeks,
I stand on my tiptoes to take a peek.

The pan is huge and filled to the top,
With crunchy veg to make this Welsh broth.

Leeks, potatoes, parsley and meat
Make the cawl a winter treat.

Chunks of crusty bread to dip,
Blow it first or it'll burn your lip.

Leeks and daffs show we're Welsh,
But it's Mum's hot Welsh cawl I love best.

Holly-Ann Yeo (8)
Lakefield Primary School, Llanelli

Cawl

First we put in the vegetables.
Second we put in the meat.
Third we put in the water.
Cook it all morning till afternoon.
Tidy and clean the whole house.
Every single room except the bathroom.
Wait till your guests come
When they eat it up.
But not me, I hate cawl, it smells like poo.
It makes your breath smell like it too.
Guests' children have been tumbling.
Oh no their bellies are rumbling.
To the bathroom they will go,
I was lucky I didn't clean the bathroom floor.

Jordan Lewis (8)
Lakefield Primary School, Llanelli

Cawl

Sshh, let's listen,
To the sound of water bubbling in the pot.
Must be careful as it's hot!
Chopping potatoes, parsnips,
Onions and carrots too,
To make enough cawl for me and you.
The table's all set with spoons and bowls,
Along with lovely buttered crunchy bread rolls.
Mmm, now it's time to eat,
The cawl warms me from my head to my feet.

Thomas Parry (7)
Lakefield Primary School, Llanelli

Holiday In Ibiza

Ibiza is warm in the sun.
All I say to my mum, 'I am having fun.'
Hooray! No school.

In the cool beach laying on the sand
I say to my dad, 'Here is a good piece of land.'
Going to the disco, in the warm night,
I'm dancing away till the dawn light.

It's time to go, leave the blue sky,
I've packed my bags, it's time to fly.
Leaving Ibiza, leaving the sea,
I wonder if they loved me!
Ibiza.

Emily Prentice-Gregory (10)
Lakefield Primary School, Llanelli

Flowers

I am like a daisy flower born in the summer of 1993.
I bloomed to be a beautiful girl with long brown hair
And big brown eyes.

I am as right as rain when I want to be
But that's mostly all the time.

I play with my friends outside
And when it is time to come in and work, I sigh and say '*Oh no!*'

I am quite a perky girl even when
I am ill at home with the flu or a bug.

I am quite an anxious girl with my work,
Most of the time anyway.

I love most of the subjects especially art
Because we can draw, paint and play with clay.

Rebecca Bello (10)
Lakefield Primary School, Llanelli

Rainbows

R ed is the first colour the eye does see
A s a rainbow appears for you and me
I ndigo is also a part of the scene
N othing can take that away from me
B eautiful colours up in the sky
O ver the lands and mountains so high
W ishing our dreams would never die.

Stacey Evans (10)
Lakefield Primary School, Llanelli

The Sound Collector
(Based on 'The Sound Collector' by Roger McGough)

A stranger called in Lakefield
Dressed all in grey and white
Put every sound into a bag
And took them out of sight
The laughing of the children
The creaking of the chair
The screaming on the yard
The shouting of the teacher
The crying of the infants
The creaking of the door
The ticking of the clock
The whirring of the pipes
The rattling of the tray
A stranger called in Lakefield
He didn't leave his name
He put all sounds into a bag
School will never be the same.

Jack Rolfe (8)
Lakefield Primary School, Llanelli

The Only One

If I had to pick a boy out of 22,
The answer is simple - I'd pick *you*.
You're the only one that can make me smile.
If you were far away, I'd run a million miles.
I'd run across gravel, stone and sand,
Just to be in the same land.
If my face had a great big frown
You're the one who would turn it upside down.
If ever I was ill during the night,
You'd text me to see if I was alright.
Because you are happy as can be -
You're the only one for me.

Alysha Gibson (11)
Lakefield Primary School, Llanelli

Cawl

Cawl is delicious, just you wait and see,
Mammy is making a pot for you and for me.
In go the potatoes, then the leeks
She always makes too much, it will last for two weeks.
Mammy says cawl is good for you,
Welsh people have been eating it for generations you see.
Dad says if it's good enough for Dewi
It's good enough for me!
Mammy adds the last of the ingredients
It's coming on a treat
It won't be long and it will be ready to eat.

Joshua Thomas (8)
Lakefield Primary School, Llanelli

Cawl

What I like best - in a bowl -
Is my mother's home-made cawl, with a bread roll.
Potatoes, carrots, swede and meat,
All boiled up for us to eat.
It's with my spoon I like to slurp,
When it's gone I have a burp.

Some people say that cawl is bad,
When they say this, I get mad.
In the winter, during a storm,
Cawl is the soup to keep you warm.
In our school on Saint David's Day,
Cawl is for dinner. Hip, hip, hooray!

Matthew Percival (11)
Lakefield Primary School, Llanelli

Ugh! Girls

'Ugh! They're girls,' was the disbelieving shout,
As the dressing room door opened and the opposition ran out.
'Perhaps they're all mascots or boys with long hair,
We'll win this one easy, they haven't got a prayer.'

The coach tells the players they haven't got a chance,
Girls should be doing cooking, gymnastics or dance.
'How do we play them? Do we tackle hard?'
And send them off to hospital, with a get well card.

The ref blows his whistle and the game it begins,
The girls aren't really bothered which team wins.
But the boys they want it badly, couldn't bear to lose
And see their names being mentioned in the local news.

The pace is very fierce with both sides giving their all,
Then up steps Samantha Thomas, with a cracking through ball.
Amy over to Jade, Jade to Heather Brown
And the next thing you know, the boys are one down.

The boys are in a panic, looking at the clock
And the coach just stands there
Holding his head in disbelief and shock.
There goes the ref's final whistle, the girls have beaten the boys,
The game is finally over, barring all the noise.
The boys are disappointed, but there's something to celebrate,
The girls have given their telephone numbers,
So they can ask them for a date.

Samantha Thomas (11)
Lakefield Primary School, Llanelli

Football

I love football,
I'm a real football fan,
I watch it on the TV
Or in the football stand.
I love Newcastle United -
They're my favourite team,
When they win I'm happy -
When they lose I'm sad.
They call us the Toon Army
Because we're really barmy.
Swansea City also rock,
Another team I like.
I've also seen them play for real,
With 8,000 screaming fans.
They won 3-0, oh what a dream!
That was a perfect night.

Alex Rothe (10)
Lakefield Primary School, Llanelli

Colours

Green, yellow, purple, red,
That's what I see when I'm in bed.
Red, purple, yellow, green,
Prettiest colours I have seen.

Blue, orange, brown and pink,
That's what I see in a sink.
Pink, brown, orange, blue,
I also love these colours too.

Casey Higgon
Lakefield Primary School, Llanelli

Music

I'm in a choir because I love to sing
And my brother plays the violin.
I'm learning the recorder - I have lessons every week,
For I like to keep the rhythm and I like to keep the beat.
I enjoy listening to music,
Music that's happy and bright.
It wakes me up in the morning
And relaxes me at night.
I love to play a melody,
And also keep the harmony.
I love to sing and lift my voice,
For music makes my heart rejoice.
Semibreves, minims, crotchets and quavers,
All types of music, with all different flavours.
Music to calm you and make you relax,
To listen to while walking or having a bath.
 M is for music - let it be heard!
 U is for universal, all around the world
 S is for soothing, to help you unwind
 I is for images it brings to your mind
 C is for creativity, music you want to make
    For you to enjoy and celebrate.

Christian Roberts (11)
Lakefield Primary School, Llanelli

Wales Is The Best

F ootball is the best
O n television or on the pitch
O ur team is put to the test
T hey are the boys in red
B all skills from foot to head
A t the Millennium Stadium we play
L et's kick it all the way
L ots of goals for *Wales*.

Dafydd Phillips (11)
Lakefield Primary School, Llanelli

Breeze

Can you hear the breeze flowing through the trees?
Can you hear the breeze howling through the leaves?
Can you hear the breeze calling your name
And whistling silently as if it's ashamed?

Can you feel the breeze blowing gently through your hair?
Can you feel the breeze flowing round you?
Can you feel the breeze trying to do something that you like to do
And looking after you like you should do too?

Yes I hear the breeze flowing through the trees,
Yes I hear the breeze howling through the leaves,
Yes I hear the breeze calling my name
And yes it does whistle silently as if it's ashamed.

Yes I feel the breeze blowing gently through my hair,
Yes I feel the breeze flowing round me,
Yes I feel the breeze trying to do something that I like to do
And looking after me like I should do too.

Amber White (10)
Llangwm VC Primary School, Haverfordwest

Band

I must go down to the band again
To the trumpet's blaring sound
And all I ask is a cheering crowd
To make noise at the end of each round.
The flutes whistle while the clarinets toot
And all to the time of the teacher's tapping boot.

I must go down to the band again
To have a lovely time
And all I ask is another song to make the day more fine
And the band begins to play as the sun goes down,
The memories we have will never make us frown.

Eleanor Ewart (10)
Llangwm VC Primary School, Haverfordwest

You Can Say

You can say
Lovely, cute, charming,
Good, enjoyable,
Friendly,
But not *nice!*

You can say
Likeable, helpful, cuddly
Fine, beautiful
Kind
But not *nice!*

Said my nice teacher.

Poppy Leggett (10)
Llangwm VC Primary School, Haverfordwest

Peace

War is full of people dying,
War is full of pilots flying.
Peace is happy, not sad,
War is wrong and bad.

War is dark and bloody,
In trenches deep, small and muddy,
Peace is beautiful and kind
And peace is hard to find.

War is terrible not kind,
Peace is nice, I'm sure you'll find,
War is mean
And war has been.

Joseph Antonie Kiff (10)
Llangwm VC Primary School, Haverfordwest

My Dog

My dog is my best friend, he's there when I need him,
He's there when I feed him.
He won't let me down
And he'll never frown.
He likes to roll in mud,
As he lands in it with a great big thud.

My dog is my best friend,
Although he chews things to bits,
He keeps me in fits.
I like to take him on walks,
Even though he never talks,
I know what he's thinking
And he's always blinking, blinking, blinking.

My dog is everyone's best friend,
His naughtiness will never end.
People laugh and smile at him,
Because he is very very dim.
He may just be a dog to you,
But he means a lot more to me than he does to you.

Maddie Rees (11)
Llangwm VC Primary School, Haverfordwest

Silly Things

A pack of peas, a pound of cheese,
Pot of jam, slice of ham,
Shiny glue, sticky shoe,
Lovely berries, crinkled cherries,
A ripe peach and some bleach.

Charlotte O'Donoghue (10)
Llangwm VC Primary School, Haverfordwest

Friends

Friends are special, friends are cool
I see my friends each day at school
We laugh and joke and play around
When we meet up in the playground

At 3.25 we get on the bus
The teacher says, 'Now don't make a fuss'
Can't wait to get home at the end of the day
To call for my friends to come out and play

Scooters and bikes are really good fun
Till I get a shout to come in from Mum
Tea and homework, bath and bed
Why can't I play with my friends *instead!*

James Griffiths (9)
Llangwm VC Primary School, Haverfordwest

Shopping List

A bottle of bubbling wine and one juicy lime,
A packet of rice and some chocolate mice,
Some red berries and a packet of cherries,
A pot of honey you'll need lots of money,
One big mop from the cleaning shop,
A ripe peach and some dangerous bleach.

Alice Edwards (9)
Llangwm VC Primary School, Haverfordwest

Mothers

Mothers who needs them?
Bossing us about around
The school out and about!

Sis and me bossed about
'Sasha what comes before U?'
'Tea?'
'Yes please! Not coffee!'

Jade get this, get that!
Get all the jewellery off
The click of the fingers
Just like that!

But on the plus side
Of her being my mum is . . .
I am the luckiest kid in the world!

Jade Berry (10)
Llanybydder Primary School, Llanybydder

Mondays

I hate Mondays because
The weekends are all over
And I wake up
With Mum shaking me.

Mondays are bad news
All we do is work, work
And the teachers telling you
To get on with your work.

Mondays - that's all it is - is work,
Maths, science, English
And history all over again
Thank goodness for home time.

Ruth Davies (9)
Llanybydder Primary School, Llanybydder

When I'm 18

When I'm 18
I would like a flashing car
A house for myself
Then I can do what I want

I would like everything new
And I want new clothes
I want, I want, I want

I want a computer
I want a silver television
I want a DVD
And a new video

I want this dream
To come true
Then everything will go
My way.

Deloni Mair Davies (10)
Llanybydder Primary School, Llanybydder

My Sister

My sister
Is a pain
She likes running
In the rain

My sister shouts
She never doubts
About anything

She never cleans
Her room
She flies on a broom.

Jordan James (10)
Llanybydder Primary School, Llanybydder

Listen

Listen to the sound
What can you hear?
The slow, cold footsteps
Of a baby deer.
Listen and you'll hear

Listen to the sound
What can you hear?
The sound of footsteps
That are coming near.
Listen and you'll hear.

Listen to the sound
What can you hear?
The sound of birds tweeting
Listen and you'll hear.

Listen to the sound
What can you hear?
The sound of trees blowing in the wind
Listen and you'll hear.

Ashley Bell (9)
Llanybydder Primary School, Llanybydder

Big Brothers

The girls that rule
My big brother tries to act cool
He tries and tries but he looks like a fool

They broke his heart
And started to laugh
He looked up and started peering
Poor little fool had nothing to do

But I am glad he is my big brother
Cos sisters are selfish and bossy.

Alice George (9)
Llanybydder Primary School, Llanybydder

A Dream

Have you had a dream
When you walk down
A stony path and you end up
In another world?
A world where there's peace and quiet
And everything's perfect.

A world where everybody
Is happy and friendly
With nobody fighting
And no wars and nobody suffers
From food and water shortages

If only this dream was true

A world where no animal is rare
And every species has many of them
A world where nobody
Hunts down animals
And cuts down trees
Where animals live.

A world where the sun shines
All the time and the birds
Sing happily in the trees
And the leaves dance in the breeze.

If only this dream was true.

A world where nobody
Throws rubbish on the ground
And you can't see wrappers
By the pavement.

A world where you
Can hear laughter
All the time,
Children playing in the park -
Picking raspberries,
Strawberries and blackberries.

If only this dream was true.

Daniella Beaumont (10)
Llanybydder Primary School, Llanybydder

When I'm Older

When I'm older
I'm going to get a wife
And lots of money
I wish I could get a car.

I might get a house
And a baby
To keep me company.
I'd get a job to keep me going.

I'd tell my dad to
Keep out of my business
And let me do what I want
But I know he'll be
Bossing me around.

If I have a boy
It will be called Scott
And if I have a girl
She will be called Chloe.
When I get a wife
She'd better be a good lady.
I will get married
And live happily ever after.

Emyr Wyn Jones (10)
Llanybydder Primary School, Llanybydder

Legolas

Longbow carrier
Elf prince
Gimli's friend
Orc slayer
Life protector
Arrow aimer
Swift runner.

Jack Cartwright (11)
Llechryd Primary School, Cardigan

Ingredients For A Rainbow

Take some red as pure as blood
Take some orange as vivid as flames
Then some yellow as acid as lemon
Take some green as bright as grass

Then some blue as dark as the ocean
Add some indigo as velvet as violets
And hey presto!
There you have it -
A rainbow for spring.

Skye Heneker (10)
Llechryd Primary School, Cardigan

What I Can Do In One Second

I can smell a flower,
I can take a deep breath,
I can take a big step,
I can kick a ball,
I can clap my hands,
I can nod my head,
I can jump in the air,
I can write a word,
I can rub out a word,
I can lick an ice cream.

Samantha Francis (9)
Llechryd Primary School, Cardigan

My Family

My mum
She's always cleaning the house
And she is scared of a mouse
She sleeps during movies
And loves drinking smoothies
That's my *mum*.

My dad
He's always in the shed
Planning the day ahead
He often combs his hair
He really doesn't care
That's my *dad*.

My brother
He always sleeps on his bed
His favourite colour is red
He hates reading books
He hasn't got the looks
That's my *brother*

Me
Well I am just perfect
That's *me*.

Angharad Rees (11)
Llechryd Primary School, Cardigan

Dolphins

D aring, dancing mammals
O bservant, ocean dwellers
L oving, likeable communicators
P layful, plunging creatures
H igh leaping animals
I mportant, imaginative life forms
N atural, neat learners
S wimmers skimming oceans!

Olivia Stewart (11)
Llechryd Primary School, Cardigan

Treasure Chest

Open the ancient chest,
Discover a tattered vest,
Pearls that glimmer,
Gold that will shimmer
And diamonds that shine in the sun.

Chains and bracelets,
Earrings and anklets
And a map covered in blankets,
A pirate's flag all covered in mould,
Touch it and you'll get a cold.

Around the chest,
A rusted lock,
Surrounded by a fierce crock,
Gold panels and rotted flannels,
And that's what's in my treasure chest.

Hayley McLaughlin (11)
Llechryd Primary School, Cardigan

My Puppy Narla

As bouncy as a ball,
As loving as a teddy,
As happy as a heart,
She's the best puppy ever.

Her coat is soft, soft silk,
Her ears are a wave of gold,
She's sleepy when we tell her, 'Bed,'
And naughty when she won't,
Narla is my puppy forever.

Amy Robinson (10)
Llechryd Primary School, Cardigan

Just Kidding

Hey Dad
Guess what?
There's an alien in the fridge
Guess what?
He ate everything
Guess what?
He bit me and it hurt
Guess what?
Fooled you
Ha ha ha

Hey Dad
Guess what?
There's an alien on the roof
Guess what?
He fell down the chimneys
Guess what?
He broke the TV
Guess what?
Fooled you

Hey Mum
Guess what?
There's an alien behind you
Guess what?
He broke the cooker
Guess what?
Fooled you
Ha ha ha ha.

Branwen Lewis (9)
Llechryd Primary School, Cardigan

Letter To A Tiger

Dear Tiger,
How long will your species be safe?
How long will your habitat be protected?

Silent hunter in the jungle,
Black and orange cat,
Prowling in the sunlight and shadows.

I hope that you will remain alive
And your fierce beauty stay with us.
Please can I help you?

From a tiger-lover called Josie.

Josie Westbury (10)
Llechryd Primary School, Cardigan

The Haunted Castle

It was a cold and gloomy night,
As the mist rose over the derelict castle
And the moon was shining bright
Over the turrets and stagnant water of the moat.

Over the rotten, mouldy drawbridge
The ghosts and spooks were hovering in every room
Haunting, howling and wailing

If you enter you're sure to meet your *doom!*

Steven Woodhouse (11)
Llechryd Primary School, Cardigan

A Day In The Life Of Pooh

Winnie the Pooh, he walks along
Singing his lovely morning song.
Then he finds he has no money
To buy his delicious, yellow honey.
So to get some honey he climbs a tree,
But poor Pooh Bear, gets stung by a bee.
He looks for Eyore, Piglet and Roo,
Owl, Tigger and Rabbit too.
Singing like they always do,
For this is a day in the life of Pooh.

Sarah Sommerville (10)
Llechryd Primary School, Cardigan

Who Made . . . ?

Who made our sun yellow,
Our big red shining star,
The gigantic fireball
That keeps us warm
And sends us light from afar?

Who made our planet blue
With water, creatures and all?
Home for many people
Living in every land
Standing proud and tall?

Hannah Sommerville (10)
Llechryd Primary School, Cardigan

The Ghostly Galleon

Cutting through the waves like a dagger in blue velvet,
The waves rippling where the ship sails are
Battered and delicately on the mast,
White horses dance on the waves,
As wind creaks through the rigging,
The black rags swing on the end of the pole.

As Captain Peg Leg uses his skeletal hands
To haul up the rigging it sways,
You can see his shining glass eye glinting in the moonlight,
His miss-match clothes sparkling with jewels,
The dark, black, matted beard plaited with blood red ribbon,
A torn pirate's hat sitting on his dark head,
The teeth he still has left are rotting and black.

Most of Captain Peg Leg's crew have black braided hair,
Their teeth are crumbling and missing,
Some of them even have an eye patch,
But all of them are covered in scars.

They speak of tales about faraway lands,
About islands and treasure maps,
Tales of how they got their scars
When they were fighting with soldiers.

Captain Peg Leg can even tell you the tale of how he lost his leg,
Some of his crew will tell about the way their eye
Was stuck to the end of an enemy's sword,
One pirate can tell a tale of how he lost all four fingers,
The stories are quite a scare.

The island where they live is surrounded by sharp rocks,
If you get onto the island past all the deadly rocks
You may find the beach golden, deserted,
Captain Peg Leg has used all the rock as cannonballs,
The island may have some empty treasure chests,
The gold is in Captain Peg Leg's beard!

Captain Peg Leg and his crew are cursed,
A terrible, skin-burning curse,
If they ever touch you, you will both fry to a bone,
So if you ever happen to see a sparkle in the distance
Or hear the sound of a drum,
Then pray for a gust of wind to carry you far, far away!

Emma Groves (10) & Megan Williams (11)
Milford Haven Junior School, Milford Haven

A Little Funny Man

I know a little funny man
As quiet as a mouse he is
He can help many people
Around every house
He hasn't been seen that much
But has such a tender touch
That's Mr Nobody

He has done a lot of damage
But never does tell
He always takes my stuff
But never owns up
He has a lot of problems
And never cleans them up
That's Mr Nobody

He brings in mud
Dirties your carpet
He reads the papers
Never puts them back
Nobody has read them
If Mum does ask
That's Mr Nobody.

Alice Brumby (11)
Milford Haven Junior School, Milford Haven

The Black Pearl!

The Pearl enters the dark oozing waters,
Her sails were tattered and torn,
The wind howled in the moonlight,
Every night the ship takes lives
With deadly guns and cannons.

Captain Blackheart captains this deadly ship,
For everyone fears his name,
He will slaughter anyone who makes fun of
The patch on his diseased eye,
His face was like a bucket of bones,
His beard was knotted and jewelled,
His teeth were yellow and rotted and that was his nasty game.

The crew were mean, keen and were ready
To make people scream,
They were more like ghostly figures
With skeletal hands in the moonlight
People say they're a legend but we think it's true.

The first sun that came out of the horizon
The ship goes out to sea, adventure is about to begin,
The sails are billowing wildly,
The skull and crossbones flying high for all to see,
They're out to find some treasure,
Their greed cheering them on,
They don't mind where they find it or who they steal from
As long as they get some they don't care at all.

The island they hide on is covered with smooth silky sand,
The treasure will hide on this luxury island,
No one will ever dare to look for this island,
For it is cursed with a deadly spell,
That's their little greedy island,
The spell they have is terrible.

The curse is upon them for all eternity,
They will conquer your homes at night
They don't know what they are doing
For the curse has cursed their minds
With deadly thoughts.
If you see them run and hide
'Ah ha me hearties'
Good luck 'cause they may come for you!

Rebecca Hearse Morgan & Lauren Owens (10)
Milford Haven Junior School, Milford Haven

Jumping

In the morning I jump out of bed,
I get up and jump over my mum's head,
I jump in the bath with my sponge ted,
I jump out, back on my bed.
I jump into my trousers, my jumper too,
I jump everywhere needing the loo.
I jump in my shoes after my socks,
I jump in my cereal then using a cloth.
I jump in the car ready for school,
I'm still jumping around needing the loo.
I jump around school my teacher asks me why I can't stop,
To speak I'm the jumping Jack, *eek!*
Oops I'm jumping so much I've bumped into teach,
I must get off, I haven't time to speak.
I jump into bed my feet feel like lead
Time to rest until I get up.

Katie Edwards (10)
Milford Haven Junior School, Milford Haven

Captain Hook's Poem

The Golden Galleon sailing across the dark and misty moonlit sea.
How silently it goes creaking all the time.
It's tough as old boots upon the dark blue sea.

Captain Hook has lots of jewels in his braided hair,
A few missing teeth and a very long beard.
He's got a hook for a hand and a wooden leg.
His eyes look as sly as a fox.
He's tall and thin, sometimes nice, sometimes not.
Who knows what will happen to you?
Pirates wear different sorts of stripes on T-shirts and on trousers.
With head scarves coloured in blue and red.
Some are tall and thin, others are small and fat.

Their adventures are stealing from rich people
And finding new and bare islands.
Sailing the Seven Seas
Finding precious gold in abandoned caves.

They steal rich clothes like velvet
And parrots like Amazon's blue and yellow.
Stealing gorgeous gold from mayors and kings,
They find a new ship. Be careful, don't get caught!

They hide out on the island of *lost souls.*
They eat coconuts from palm trees.
It looks nice but believe you me it is not.
There's a sunken ship with chest and bones.
Beware!

Captain Hook picked up a coin as gold as the sunshine
Shining so bright.
He didn't know it was a curse
Of the flying Dutchman.

If you hear a 'Yo ho ho' beware beware beware!
If you see a pirate or a pirate ship called the Golden Galleon
Run, run as fast as you can.

Elinor Roberts & Julie Potter (10)
Milford Haven Junior School, Milford Haven

The Black Pearl

White whipped waves hit the ghostly ship,
Dusty decks drag apart,
Sheets of sails, fly away on the darkened sea,
Winds whipping against the battered ship,
Golden tables rock back and forth the ship.

Growling under his smelly doggy breath,
Grunting commands by Captain Black,
Captain's golden eyes reflect the sun,
Captain Black's splintered wooden leg scrapes the deck,
Silver buttons on the stolen navy coat.

Shattering bones of his crew,
Bony fingers as you touch,
Pointed hats just like witches,
Sword so sharp they will cut straight through you.

He sails the world like a Roman emperor,
Rough seas as Captain Black's crew sail the Seven Seas.

Torturing everyone, everywhere,
Thieving sparkling jewels,
Raiding places, destroying homes,
Enjoying themselves as exciting adventures begin.

Their gruesome hideout,
Where nobody thinks they can live,
With sparkling jewels,
With flowing rivers,
With huge bloody palm trees,
Where they can see who is coming.

Curses they love 'em,
Makes them strong and gruesome,
They are skeletons by night,
If you hear or see them in the distance,
Run for your life Captain Black's on your back,
So be afraid!

Samantha Booth (11) & Jessica Thomas (10)
Milford Haven Junior School, Milford Haven

The Ghostly Galleon

Out of the darkness appears The Black Pearl
Filled with a crew of scavengers.
The ripped sail blows in the misty wind
And cannons roar and thunder through the night.
The sails are badly damaged from all the bloody battles.

The captain has one bloodshot eye, covered in a patch
That has a terrifying skull in the middle.
He wears a tall, red hat with a black button at the back.
He's got a wooden leg and a tattoo of a Jolly Roger
On his muscle-bound arm.
His cutlass shines in the moonlight like a jewel.

They were a motley crew who would make anyone
Walk the long, lonely plank for trying to steel their booty.
They had few rotten, yellowing teeth but plenty of scars
Won from the many battles they'd had.

The Black Pearl had sailed the Seven Seas leaving unlucky
Boats to sink to a watery grave.
Captain Long Leg and his motley crew would use any
Dastardly trick to get what they wanted.
His favourite, most nasty trick was to lure ships in,
Under a flag of sickness, thinking they would help.
But when they were aboard, Captain Long Leg
And his men would capture them to rot in the brig.

When Captain Long Leg needed a hard earned break
From this pirateering, The Black Pearl would slink
Into harbour on Skull Island - a swamp-infested island
Full of bloodthirsty crocodiles and deadly snakes
Slithering down the sinewy branches.
A dark, dank cave is where they hide their rum
With quicksand to ward off predators be they man or beast.

They have a curse, a terrifying curse to change them into
Living skeletons - alive but fleshless.
Captain Long Leg and his crew are doomed to roam
The roaring seas never to find rest.
Only a princess' ruby red blood spilt on a mysterious moonlit night,
Over skeletal hands, will end their lonely *wandering.*

Jack Warby (10)
Milford Haven Junior School, Milford Haven

Pirates At Sea

The terrible waves splashing on the ship,
Creepy ghosts talking in the background.
The wind howling in our dirty ears
The boat tipping side to side
As we cross the Seven Seas.

Pirate Pete was his name
Who had a metal dirty hook
He is creepy and sly
Who always wants to win
He has only one eye
Which is red and gleamy

The crew were as ugly as toads
They were smelly and moaned constantly
Their teeth were rotten and yellow
And had plenty of scars

Their adventures were creepy and scary
With all blood flesh over the rocks
As they crossed the Seven Seas
With waves and sharks with gleaming teeth they passed
Through a tunnel with skulls the size of enormous rocks
With creepy crawlies and slugs
The last adventure was always getting back to the ship.

Their island is in the middle of nowhere
With only a couple of people
Pirate Pete grabbed some rum
Out of a tree with his hook
They hide out in a little camp
With jewels and gold

If you hear a 'Yo ho ho'
Run away because
That is the pirate at sea
The curse is hitting people
And putting warts on their noses
So beware before they get you.

Niall Day & Andrew Smith (10)
Milford Haven Junior School, Milford Haven

Us Pirates

The ghostly ship sailed slowly, slyly, spookily,
Across the dead blood sea the mist slowly, slowly
Surrounds us pirates on the ghost ship
Nothing but the sound of the dead blood sea
Slapping and splashing against the side of the ghost ship.

Our captain is called Captain Jack
He has one arm with a metal hook
His creepy looks turn into ghosts,
His gold and rotten teeth shine in the moonlight.
A skull and crossbones are our captain's best thing
Don't try to take them or you will get killed.

Us fearless crew march round and round
Waiting for somebody to walk the plank!
Our jewels light up the ship,
Our bandannas are red from the blood of men.
The adventure has started beware of the cutlasses!
We raise the torn sails for the gusty swirly wind
To blow us away over the raging sea
Whooshing and pushing until we capsize
Abandon ship! Abandon ship!

We reach our tropical island
The blazing hot sun shining
Shimmering and sparkling in the bright blue sky
Sweat dripping down my nose drip, drip, drip.
Then I can smell the sweet smell of all our fruits
Pineapples, bananas, coconuts and kiwis.

Our plan is to steal a ship, sail over the golden sea,
North to capture the kings of England's soldiers
Kill them and make them suffer, steal the gold,
Red rubies, crystals and emeralds.
The captain has found the other secret treasure map
Now we will be filthy rich!

Abby Wheeler & Jordan Reynolds (10)
Milford Haven Junior School, Milford Haven

Pirate Poem

The creaky eerie ship
Sails the misty seas,
With all the pirates on the ship,
Doing what they want,
The skull and crossbones flag is flying high.

The captain is the boss,
He wears black, blood-stained trousers,
A hook for a hand, shiny and sharp like a knife,
A patch covers his diseased eye,
Skull and crossbones on his big black hat,
His sword razor sharp, flashing in the sun.

This is the ghostly crew,
Always listening to the prisoners screaming,
They like to have some rum,
They're always on the lookout for a ship to plunder.

The pirates plunder east, west, north and south,
Stealing treasure from every ship,
Living a life of violence and crime,
A chest full of glittering, sparkling jewels,
An adventure as thrilling as a roller coaster,
Got the maps to find the treasure,
Walking the plank, falling in the sea as cold as ice.
Sword fighting as noisy as a jet.

The island is near,
It has palm trees as tall as mountains,
The sea lapping the shore is as blue as the sky,
The pirates hear monkeys flying through the trees,
A sandy beach is as yellow as daffodils.

If you hear or see a pirate,
Look out your skin will disappear,
Your nose will grow like a carrot,
The pirates' curse will make them
Sleep for a hundred years or more,
They will have to walk 'the plank of shame'.

Rhiannon Hobbs (10)
Milford Haven Junior School, Milford Haven

The Orange Borange

Nothing rhymes with orange it's quite annoying too!
But I know a little story I think I'll share it with you.
In a cave not far away a monster is what you'll find!
I call it the Orange Borange but it's quite friendly mind!
It likes to feed on purple furples delicious birds they are,
But the Borange could catch them in a flash,
Those furples won't get very far.
The Borange likes to drive around in his big bright orange jeep
And he drives to a hidden place where his family he will meet.
Well I guess you should know now I guess I've told you too,
But the only ones who really know are obviously me and you.

Sam Freeman (11)
Milford Haven Junior School, Milford Haven

Winter!

Freezing air
City breaks
Cold air blows
Under slates.

Slates fall off
In the snow
Umbrellas blow
Trees snap.

Lips freeze
Scarves on
Winter's here
Once again.

Bradley James Cristofaro (9)
Milford Haven Junior School, Milford Haven

Mums

My mum is great
But she is always late to pick you up
She likes to chatter, chatter, chatter
And when she eats chocolate
She gets fatter, fatter, fatter
My mum is great because she
Takes care of me and Nia
My mum does the cooking
My mum does the cleaning
My dad doesn't because he burns the fish fingers
And he doesn't do the cleaning
Because he will clean the wrong thing
With the wrong thing
This means mums are the *best.*

Libby Wheeler Smith (9)
Milford Haven Junior School, Milford Haven

In The Park

In the park I play and play,
On lots and lots of summer days.

Slide, slide, slide,
I watch the birds glide.

Bring, bring, bring,
Some bike bells ring.

Babies are crying, children are playing,
Mums are chattering, horses are neighing,
Dogs are barking, cats are miaowing,
Fishes are swimming in the pond,
Lots of people are really fond.
More people come
And have lots of fun.

Bethan Busby (9) & Emily Brock (10)
Milford Haven Junior School, Milford Haven

Rainbow

Once I saw a rainbow,
Hanging in the sky,
But to see it,
I had to lift my head up high.

Once I saw a rainbow,
Glistening at me,
My family and I saw it,
While we were eating tea.

Once I saw a rainbow,
Shining very bright,
I thought it was a UFO,
So it did give me a fright!

Once I saw a rainbow,
As pretty as it could be,
I was looking at it so much,
I fell and hurt my knee!

Once I saw a rainbow,
Disappear at a snail's pace,
Suddenly it had gone
And there were tears coming down my face.

Goodbye rainbow,
See you again next time
When the sun and clouds come out to play,
When it rains or shines!

Alexandra Othen (10)
Milford Haven Junior School, Milford Haven

Winter Is Here

Frosty night
Dull and dark
In warm clothes eating dinner
Warm soup yum yum!

Snow on top of cars
Icy roads
Milford Haven best of all

Bedtime up to bed
Get into bed, warm up
Then wake up to another day
When you do it all again.

Jessica Whitby (9)
Milford Haven Junior School, Milford Haven

Sophie's Dragon Poem

In China they have dragons
They live in wagons
The dragons blew fire
They also would tire
They were colourful
And also quite beautiful
Dragons are sometimes fierce
But also cry tears
I wish one day I could see for myself.

Sophie Williams (8)
Milford Haven Junior School, Milford Haven

If I Were A . . .

If I were a dog, I'd skip around,
If I were a dog, I'd dig holes in the ground.

If I were a dog I'd like to play,
If I were a dog, I'd use the litter tray.

I remember seeing a dog,
He was all fluffy and cuddly,
He ran across the beach with a log,
The sand was all golden and puddly.

If I were a dog, I'd play with a ball,
If I were a dog, I'd like going to the mall.

If I were a dog, I'd be black and white,
If I were a dog, I'd sleep outside at night.

I remember meeting a dog,
I smoothed his blond furry head,
On his collar it said his name was Mog,
'Careful, he'll lick you,' his owner said.

If I were a dog I'd lick your hand,
If I were a dog I'd play with an elastic band.

If I were a dog I'd give you a fright,
If I were a dog I'd like to fly a kite.

I remember stroking a dog,
His fur was nice and smooth,
He ran away into the fog,
Oh, that dog could move!

So it's quite obvious that I like dogs,
I wish I had one myself,
But my mum said that dogs are like hogs
And that he'd eat all the cat food himself.

Cathy Eaton (9)
Milford Haven Junior School, Milford Haven

Winter

People go outside,
freezing cold.
Wrap up warm
in the snow.

Ice on floor,
slip, slop, slap.
Hurt yourself
on the wall.

Snowballs thrown,
snowmen build.
Time for tea,
let's go in.

Gone inside,
play some games.
Have some tea,
you and me.

Go to bed,
sleep again.
Dream until
another day.

Harley Nicholas (8)
Milford Haven Junior School, Milford Haven

Kitty

It's just a pity
I have no kitty
She died just a few weeks ago
Her name was . . . oh I don't know
It's just a pity to see her go.

Callum O'Donovan (8)
Milford Haven Junior School, Milford Haven

The Washing Machine Monster

There's a monster in my washing machine
He eats my socks and underpants.
There's nothing I can do with him
The washing machine monster.

I was going out one night
To the cinema with friends
My top was in the wash
But then the monster attacked.

I was late for school one day
Cos I couldn't find my socks
I thought they were in the basket
But the washing machine monster ate them;

You will never ever see him
He hides when you open the door
But I try to catch a peek
At the washing machine monster.

Naomi Wild (11)
Milford Haven Junior School, Milford Haven

The Spring Magic

Spring is for the lonely flowers
Sunshine blazing through the window
Easter is coming very soon
The rabbit is coming tonight.

Martyn White (10)
Milford Haven Junior School, Milford Haven

Winter

Go for a walk down the street,
Lots of snow lots of sleet.
In the gutter some slush,
A winter walk is so lush.

The winter wind is chilly,
The children outside are being silly.
They all dress up warm,
There might be a storm.
They all run inside in a second.

Dylan Larsen (9) & Ross Sutton (8)
Milford Haven Junior School, Milford Haven

Winter

Frozen ground
Deep snow
It's all around
There's nowhere to go!

Lips are sore
Noses red
Now we're inside
Let's go back to bed!

Cold outside
Trees are bare
Icy lake
Freezing air.

Tamsin Mathias (8)
Milford Haven Junior School, Milford Haven

The Poem That Makes No Sense

Am I the weirdest of the lot?
Do they like me or do they not?
Are they dumb or are they unkind?
Or maybe I am falling behind.
Do you see that person there?
Come over here and have a stare.
Now you know what I feel like,
Even if you've stole my bike.
I'm the one who stands out in class,
Some people say I cannot pass.
Sometimes I have no friends,
My life just twists, turns and bends.
Now you know this poem makes no sense,
When I wrote it I was tense.

Jade Sims (10)
Milford Haven Junior School, Milford Haven

The Dark Night

The dark night drops to the ground
Like a boulder from the sky
The headlamps of cars and motorbikes
Don't forget street lights
Like a murky brown
Through the mists of change
A boy is exchanged
For a penny in a lane.

Gaynor Jeffries (10)
Milford Haven Junior School, Milford Haven

Jungle In The House

The dog is in the oven,
The cat is in the bin,
The fish is in the toilet
And the mouse is in the tin.

The rhino is in my bed,
The shark's taking a bath,
The spider's in the microwave
And the roach is on my toy giraffe.

The elephant's in my garden shed,
The snake is on my mum's bra,
The bear is in the fridge
And, oh! The lions are on the new car!
What a jungle!

Rhiannon Mathias (10)
Milford Haven Junior School, Milford Haven

Dance Of Light

Dance around the candlelight,
Candle burning oh so bright.
Quick step honey let's not fight,
Let's dance together to put out the light.

Light still burning oh so bright,
Let's learn together to share the light.
Dance together so full of joy,
Candle burning oh boy, oh boy.

Friends of the dance school team together,
Lifting, swirling and pulling together.
Rhythm and music oh so loud,
Lights are glistening all around.

Alisha John (10)
Milford Haven Junior School, Milford Haven

Going To The Welsh Assembly

M y trip to the Welsh Assembly,
I nteresting and exciting
C hatting to my mates on the way
H earing the assembly members talking
A t half past twelve we had our lunch
E ating our sandwiches and crisps
L unchtime ended at twenty to one

H urrying to see the chamber
I ncredibly large it is
R ushing to get seats on the bus
E verything we did today, was absolutely fantastic.

Michael Hire (7)
Milford Haven Junior School, Milford Haven

Sea Days

A big grey dog,
Stood on a cliff
Howling at the moon and . . .

A rough sea,
Spilling over the sides of boats,
Rolling waves crashing against cliffs and rocks but . . .

A calm sea scarcely snores,
On quiet days of May or June,
No people to make a noise,
To mix with the tune of the wind,
Calmly blowing.

Siôn Littlehales (11)
Milford Haven Junior School, Milford Haven

My Cat

I have a cat
Who's round and fat
He never wants to play
He just sleeps away the day

He likes to eat fish
From his very own dish
Then he settles down
To wash fur of silky brown

He's out all night
Comes back quite a sight
God knows where he's been
Now he needs a good clean

After a drink of milk
His fur now of silk
He curls up on my lap
For a well earned nap.

Abbie George (8)
Milford Haven Junior School, Milford Haven

My Dragon Poem

I have a dragon
His name is Phil
His favourite game is fireball
He talks to me before I sleep
In the morning he makes me breakfast
He goes everywhere with me
Sometimes I get to ride on him
He makes letters in the sky with smoke
When he lands he goes to sleep.

Josh Kenniford (8)
Milford Haven Junior School, Milford Haven

Over The Hills

Over the hills and far away
There is a place where I'd love to play,
So many flowers, so many trees,
Blowing gently in the summer breeze.

The butterflies dance up in the sky
And the golden sun shines way up high.
The bees are humming and the birds are singing
And in the distance bells are ringing.

There's a beautiful pond with swans afloat
And a tiny little fishing boat.
There's boys playing football
And a boy with a kite,
It's all very perfect, such a wonderful sight.

But it is a dream
And not really there today,
Over the hills
And *too* far away.

Ben Davies (8)
Milford Haven Junior School, Milford Haven

My Chinchilla

My chinchilla is like a big fluffy ball,
In fact he looks like a snowball.
He runs and jumps like he's doing gymnastics
And when you try to kiss him he gives you a lick.
His nickname is Crunchy,
Because his nuts he likes to crunch.
He likes to sleep in the day,
But then at night he wants to play.
I love my little fluffy ball,
Because he's my little fellow.

Alex Carter (8)
Milford Haven Junior School, Milford Haven

My Teacher

Miss Thomas is my teacher's name
She likes to take us for PE and games
When all our work is done we listen to a tape
And then look at bones of different shapes.

She helps us with our reading books
And when we're writing she'll have a look
To make sure all is going well
And help us with words we cannot spell.

I like being in Miss Thomas' class
And I'll be sorry when this year has passed
For now I'll just enjoy the fun
And hope to see her in years to come.

Lauren Picton (7)
Milford Haven Junior School, Milford Haven

The Lady In Bloom

The lady in bloom
Is as red as a rose
And as sweet as
Our eyes can see.

The lady in bloom
Has a gold but pure heart
And is beautiful as can be.

Oh I wish I could be
Like the lady in bloom
Who is sweet, calm and kind
She's someone that if
You looked for years
You'd never ever find.

Verity White (11)
Milford Haven Junior School, Milford Haven

Winter

Snow is falling glittering white,
People say what a beautiful sight!
Play on snowboards, shout with glee,
Mum is calling in for tea!

By the fire,
Eating mince pies,
Looking outside at the dark skies!

'Time for bed,' Mum said,
Wake up in the morn
I'll get up before dawn!

Cheyenne Butler (8)
Milford Haven Junior School, Milford Haven

Bumblebee

Look at us we're bumblebees
Buzzing around
Not stopping to have
A rest on the ground.
In the flowers out we pop
And then we get stuck
In a lollipop.
Riggle riggle out we come
We have a race
Hey I won
Then get in my bed
And rest my head.

Abby Wheeler & Rebecca Algieri (11)
Milford Haven Junior School, Milford Haven

Hamsters

Hamsters are very funny,
They're also very sweet and fluffy,
They're also very good for keeping you company,
They'll keep you from going moany,
But watch out if you've got a cat,
If it tries to get it, just hit it with a mat,
They can be long or short haired,
Just find which looks better when compared,
They can also be fat or thin,
Whichever one, their claws are as sharp as a pin.

Jonathan Craig (10)
Milford Haven Junior School, Milford Haven

A Pirate's Life

I am a pirate from far away
With rum and brandy I travel every day
I come with my fellow hearties
I love to drink beer at parties
My ship is feared wherever it sails
Of my crew they tell dark, dark tales.

I have a patch over my eye
But with my other I can spy
I have a beard
My crew is feared.

The Jolly Roger is our flag
Of daring deeds we love to brag
Battles fought, treasures won
Being a pirate is so much fun
This is a story from Captain Slater
Have to go, see you later.

Erin Smith (11)
Milford Haven Junior School, Milford Haven

Schooldays

I get up every morning half past seven, quarter to eight,
I've got to get ready quick, I must not be late.
I get into school and I open my tray,
'Mmm, what work have I got to do today?'
Then Miss walks in the classroom and sits at her desk,
Trying to look her very most suitable best.
Then she opens a drawer and takes out the register,
She calls out our names to number 24, then . . .
Somebody came and knocked on the door and said,
'If you don't mind this letter is for one of our band members,
It's due back on the 4th of December.'
Twenty to eleven struck on the clock,
We all hurried out the door like a big, huge flock.
Then we went out to play, had some fun, 'Ring, ring, ring,'
Sang the bell, suddenly Mr Beardsmore said, 'You can go in 6L!'
Went to maths, at the end of our lesson, we played a game
(Finger squash) Guess what, my best mate was the winner
'Oh look at the time, next is dinner!'
After dinner went back to class and sat down!
Verity then asked, 'Can Elizabeth help me look after 4M?'
And Miss said, 'Of course she can.'
Skip a few hours, now it's quarter past three,
I'm going home now, *yippee!*

Elizabeth Tamilia (10)
Milford Haven Junior School, Milford Haven

Sunset Over Sea

The sun is a beautiful thing
It fills the sky with light beam rays
Birds fly towards it like it's their home
As chicks cry with hunger
It has blinding colours of yellow, orange and red
Lighting the sky with a pinky glow as it
Sets across the sea

But these light beam rays dance, shimmer
And dazzle across the rippling waves
Like the poem said before,
As it sets across the sea and on me.

Lauren Littlehales (9)
Milford Haven Junior School, Milford Haven

Band Time!

Noisy time!
Drum time!
Trumpet time!
Sax time!
Flute time!
Rock 'n' roll
Twist and shout
That's what it is
All about!
Sharps and flats
Highs and lows
Up and down
We all go!
Sing and clap
Dance and shout
That's what it's
All about in our band!

Gabrielle Swales (9)
Milford Haven Junior School, Milford Haven

A Hand In The Band

Every time I play the cello
People really start to bellow

Every time I play the flute
People start to throw fruit

Every time I play on the drum
People really think I'm dumb

And every time I'm in the band
I really need a helping hand.

Hannah Jenkins (8)
Milford Haven Junior School, Milford Haven

My Family

My sister is called Helen,
She is always annoying me,
She hits me and punches a lot,
In politeness she'd get a D.

My brother is called Robert,
He likes playing a lot of games,
His favourites are football and rugby
And he wants to play for Wales.

My mother is called Catherine,
She does most of the cleaning,
She likes washing and ironing,
When my room is a mess her head hits the ceiling.

My father is called Steven,
He likes driving big machines,
He's very tall and wide
And his favourite food is beans.

Emma While (11)
Nant-Y-Groes Primary School, Ammanford

My Family

I live with my mum and dad
And they say I'm very bad.
I have a sister as well,
When you go to her door
You have to ring the bell.
I have a cat called Pickles
Who loves to have tickles,
I have four fish,
My father wants to put them on his dish.
My father owns some lorries
And he likes to go on a jolly.
When there's a mess my mother goes off her trolley,
I like lollies my sister likes sweets,
But my mother never buys these treats.

Shaun Williams (10)
Nant-Y-Groes Primary School, Ammanford

Sian My Horse

Sian is my loveable, four-legged friend,
But she can sometimes drive me round the bend.
She is kind at heart,
That's why we're never apart.

As red as a lion's mane,
She really does drive my sister insane.
I love her, she loves me,
It's really quite plain for all to see.

She is nimble and quick,
She really isn't thick.
She is brainy and brave
And I'm pretty sure she thinks I'm her slave.

As cute as a baby,
She's the best horse in the world (maybe).
So now you've heard about Sian my loveable friend.

Helen While (11)
Nant-Y-Groes Primary School, Ammanford

Rugby

Rugby is a man's game
and it's the coolest name.
The ball goes over the post,
I'm so fast the grass starts to roast.

When we go down in the scrum,
my tummy starts to rum.
We push as hard as we can
and then we have some fun.

When the ball comes out
they know we're about.
When we score a try,
we all shout high.

When the ref blows the whistle for the end,
we are still good friends.
We go back and change,
then we rearrange.

Robert While (9)
Nant-Y-Groes Primary School, Ammanford

My Family

Rhys is my brother,
He's exactly like my mother.
He moans all the time,
But he helped me with this rhyme.

Alan is my father,
He likes to eat food,
But it's chips he would rather.

Elinor is my mother, she likes to cook,
And she likes to read her book.

Sioned is my name,
Singing is my game and I like sweets,
They are really good treats.

Sioned Roberts (10)
Nant-Y-Groes Primary School, Ammanford

The Best Family

My mum is so kind,
My dad is so funny
My sister is so caring,
My brother is so playful,
My rabbit is so cute,
My fish are so colourful.
Oh, I love them so much!

My family is so nice,
I'd rather them than mice.
Especially my mum and dad,
They are so loving and caring.
I love my brother and sister too,
Although sometimes I think they should be kept in a zoo.

As for my pets, they can be pests,
But I love them so much!

Rachel Hall (10)
Nant-Y-Groes Primary School, Ammanford

My Great Mother

My great mother is the best around,
She's very responsible and kind,
Very helpful she is,
When I'm sad she can read my mind,
My mother has much faith in others,
She likes to help me out,
She's better than any other mother,
She makes a nice cup of tea,
For my sister and me.

Emyr Griffiths (10)
Ponthenri Primary School, Llanelli

My Greatest Leader

My mum is so happy and kind,
I am always on her mind.
My mother is organised and bright,
My mother is my guiding light.
She always shows she cares,
Her greatest point is that she shares.
My mother has faith and respect for all,
She's always there when I fall.
My mum is the very best,
She is better than all the rest.

Nicholas Elms (10)
Ponthenri Primary School, Llanelli

My Mother

My mum so responsible and kind,
She is always on my mind,
My mum is honest and trustworthy in my eyes,
Full of love, she is such a surprise,
Patience she shows to me,
She is the best mum that could ever be,
My mum is always approachable,
Not to mention reliable,
I love my mum,
I'll always do the best I can.

Scott Lewis (10)
Ponthenri Primary School, Llanelli

Super Mum

She's a mum that really cares,
In her heart she always shares.
Shows patience and so honest is she,
Always as busy as a bee.

She's so good to me and my brother,
She's so reliable she's better than any other.
She's so sweet and approachable,
Trustworthy, respectful and reliable.

Kisses and cuddles she always does give,
In her arms I'll always live.

Mickaela Regola (9)
Ponthenri Primary School, Llanelli

My Loving Mum

My mum is so kind,
She can read my mind.
When she is sad,
She can be mad.
But I know she cares,
As she's always willing to share.
She can be as busy as a bee,
Helpful and loving towards me.

Kayleigh Owen-Jones (11)
Ponthenri Primary School, Llanelli

My Big Sister

My sister likes to raise morale,
When I'm sad she calls me her pal,
She's hardworking and likes to care,
But she's really fussy about her hair,
She always listens really well,
When I do something naughty she doesn't tell,
Patience she shows towards me,
She's the best sister that can ever be.

Leah Johnson (9)
Ponthenri Primary School, Llanelli

My Brother And I

My brother and I help each other,
We are quite a team together,
He is so caring forever he's sharing,
He is reliable and kind,
Helps me organise my mind,
Happy, honest and hardworking,
But so awful is his singing,
But I love him very much,
He does have the golden touch.

Luke Emanuel (10)
Ponthenri Primary School, Llanelli

Blitz

Hiding under my small kitchen table in my dark house,
Sheltering from the terrible, unearthly bombing in the sky,
With mum and my frightened dog Nell,
Witnessing people screaming and running,
Bombs exploding, burning and destroying,
Buildings collapsing, crumbling and vanishing,
Listening to people screaming, yelling and shrieking,
Plane engines droning and whining above me,
Bombs exploding as they fall,
Smelling smoke, fire and dust,
Clutching my red gas mask,
Gripping the table leg tightly,
Yelling for my mum and Nell,
Feeling devastated at the horror of the bombs.

Nick Smith (8)
Roch Community School, Haverfordwest

I Wish

I wish I could feel the summer sun setting.
I wish I could see the moon's dust at night.

I wish I could see the song of the sweet robin,
I wish I could see the wind on a cold winter's day.

I wish I could hear the flowers growing in the garden,
I wish I could hear ice melt in my drink.

I wish I could touch the silver stars at night.
I wish I could touch a forest's freshness.

I wish I could see water evaporating into the sky.
I wish I could see past the horizon.

Steven Cristofaro (11)
Roch Community School, Haverfordwest

The Magic Box
(Based on 'Magic Box' by Kit Wright)

I will put in the box . . .
A frozen sea sparkling like an ice rink,
A flame of the sun's fire,
The Earth lit by moonlight.

I will put in the box . . .
A vampire with a shadow,
A 24 day year,
20 wishes that never run out.

I will put in the box . . .
The first word of a baby,
The last word of a Roman soldier,
The voice of an ancient mummy.

Billy Brockbank (10)
Roch Community School, Haverfordwest

I Wish

I wish I could hear the dew as it
drops on the grass,
I wish I could hear the sand
rolling in the crashing sea,
I wish I could hear the tables
sleeping in the dark,
I wish I could hear fish
darting through the sea,
I wish I could touch the twinkling stars
in the night sky,
I wish I could touch the hot blazing summer sun.

Rhys Quigley (11)
Roch Community School, Haverfordwest

I Wish

I wish I could hear the sand
being dragged back by the sea,

I wish I could touch the glowing stars
glistening in the night sky,

I wish I could see the cackle of a fire
on a cold winter's day,

I wish I could hear the calm water
sloshing on the cliff face,

I wish I could paint the music
of a thrush,

I wish I could paint the sound
of the trees swaying in the breeze,

I wish I could touch a cloud,
floating in the sky,

I wish I could hear the glass
in the windowpane.

Jessica Durham (10)
Roch Community School, Haverfordwest

Me - Haiku

Skateboarding down a
hill, breeze giving me a boost,
Tummy spinning round.

Andrew Ash (10)
Roch Community School, Haverfordwest

Letter To A Storm

Dear Storm,
Why do you tear down trees as though they're pieces of paper?
Why do you sink ships with your strong winds?
Why do you growl at the flaring lightning every time it flashes?
Why do you bring down power lines and leave us in the dark?
Why do you cause tidal waves and wreck homes by the sea?
Why do you make rain bucket down and maybe cause a flood?
Why do you smash windows and turn over cars?
Why do you destroy crops and rip them off their roots?
    I hope these questions make you think,
    Tell me why next time you come.

Rebecca Mountstephens (9)
Roch Community School, Haverfordwest

I Wish

I wish I could hear the shimmering stars
Flying in the sky,

I wish I could hear the brain-freezing ice cream
Flashing in the sun,

I wish I could hold a cheerful bird's voice
Echoing in the wind,

I wish I could see the gentle breeze
Brush against the trees,

I wish I could touch the dazzling sun
Just before he goes to sleep,

I wish I could hear the clouds
Fluttering in the summer sky,

I wish I could touch the sparkling moon
Singing happily in space.

James Riddiford (10)
Roch Community School, Haverfordwest

Letter To A Storm

Dear Storm,
Why do you lash down with rain on our villages?
Why do you strike lightning on our tall towering trees?
Why does your almighty power blow our plant pots over?
Why do you give us big black thundery clouds?
Why does your thunder roar like a lion?
Why do you make long black streaks far across the sky?
Why do you hammer and howl so loudly against our windows?
    Please respond on a windy day.

Abbie James (10)
Roch Community School, Haverfordwest

I Wish

I wish to paint thunder the second it strikes,
To feel autumn leaves crunch under my feet,
To hear shells scream with fright as
Waves crash over them,
To smell rain as it hits the road,
To taste a sunbeam on my tongue,
To paint waves when they crash on
Soft beige sand,
To smell the trickling water
Running down the stream,
To see the wind rushing past
As if it was late,
To hear the scorching sun crackle,
To hear a melting snowman
Sizzle in the sun,
To taste a blue flame of fire,
To be who I am.

Louis Hudson (10)
Roch Community School, Haverfordwest

The Window

Long ago there was a crooked, dusty window,
hidden away in a haunted castle.

One day a dwarf looked in the window
and saw himself as a grown man.

A zombie looked through the window
and saw a spooky grave.

A vampire looked through the window
and saw a dusty old coffin.

A giant looked through the window
and saw a leafy beanstalk.

A witch looked through the window
and saw her broom had been stolen.

A wizard looked through the window
and saw his spell exploding into bubbles.

A gargoyle looked through the window
and saw himself being freed from his rock.

A ghost looked through the window
and saw nothing . . .

Bethan O'Shea (10)
Roch Community School, Haverfordwest

Letter To A Storm

Dear Storm,
Why do you ruin buildings?
Why do you wreck trees?
Why do you wreck cars?
Why do you keep people awake?
Why do you blow the slates off churches?
Please respond.

Rhys Williams (9)
Roch Community School, Haverfordwest

Letter To A Storm

Dear Storm,
Why do you squash everything like a troll on a trampoline?
Why do you violently cause fires like an unruly group of vandals
And let the smoke zoom into the air as if it were lunging at a bird?
Why do you give the birds a fright as you flash out from the night?
Why do you strip the trees so bare like a dog you give the fox a scare?
Why do you go where everyone's banned
And in war fly over no man's land?
Why do you bust cars, houses and trees?
Why do you kill innocent bumblebees?
You're really determined to make us cry?
Thanks very much and please reply.

Ben Ford (9)
Roch Community School, Haverfordwest

I Want

I want to smell the feathers of a bird
As it flies over the glistening sea.

I want to taste the howling wind
As it races past the towering trees.

I want to hear a snowflake falling through the sky,
Whispering to his friend.

I want to smell the skin of a dolphin,
As she swims and jumps into the air.

I want to taste the laughter of a child,
As his friend tells a funny joke.

I want to hear the sun shining,
As he heats up with red-hot anger.

Alex Alderwick (11)
Roch Community School, Haverfordwest

The Magic Box
(Based on 'Magic Box' by Kit Wright)

I will put in my box . . .
The first beat of my mother's heart,
The cry of a newborn baby and
A spirit that will last forever.

I will put in my box . . .
The voice of the wind swirling in the breeze,
A swish of a tail from the Loch Ness monster,
The first violet tear from a baby dolphin.

I will put in my box . . .
A bag full of fluffy clouds
Floating on a summer's morning,
The first pink snowflake falling from a cold winter's sky,
The first bright twinkling star drifting from the midnight sky.

I shall put in my box . . .
A tenth planet in the solar system,
A bag full of second chances and a new language.

My box is silver with twinkling, colourful stars,
Open the box and bags full of secrets spill out.

Laura Rogers, Katherine Smith & Rhian McConville (10)
Roch Community School, Haverfordwest

Letter To A Storm

Dear Storm,
Why do you growl so loudly?
Why are you determined to keep us awake at night?
Why do you send lightning on trees?
Why do you clatter and destroy our slates?
Why are you so fierce and angry?
Why do you send hailstones so hard?
Why do you cover the sky with a grey blanket?
Please respond on the wind.

Megan Jenkins (8)
Roch Community School, Haverfordwest

Letter To A Storm

Dear Storm,
Why do you scare little boys and girls?
Why do you set trees on fire like a bonfire?
Why do you destroy houses and farms?
Why do you scare cats and dogs?
Why do you cut down power lines so then there's no light?
Why do you light up the sky with your zig-zaggy lines?
Why do you make it rain and hail?
Why do you growl like a lion?
Why do you make the sky an inky colour?
Why do you roll dustbins down the street like they're running away?
    Please reply.

Josh Watts (9)
Roch Community School, Haverfordwest

Letter To A Storm

Dear Storm,
Why do you make houses go on fire?
Why do you destroy the Earth?
Why do you smash windows with forked lightning?
Why do you make torrential rainfall?
Why does thunder make such an echo?
Why do you hurt and kill people?
Why do you make hailstones clatter against the window?
Why do you frighten cats and dogs with thunder?
Why do you blow dustbins with your mighty power?
    Please respond.

James George (9)
Roch Community School, Haverfordwest

A Letter To The Storm

Dear Storm,
Why do you clatter mailboxes?
Why do you create floods whooshing down the street?
Why do you make gusts of wind follow us when we run?
Why do you block roads with your fiercesome floods?
Why do you harm oak, ash and horse chestnut trees?
Why do you make street animals flee to take shelter?
Why do you throw buckets of hail which tap at our windows?
Why do you keep us awake at night?
Why do you blast off the doors and roofs of our houses?
Please respond when the third strike of lightning hits the ground.

Jodie Jones (9)
Roch Community School, Haverfordwest

Letter To A Storm

Dear Storm,
Why do you destroy trees and close loads of roads?
Why do you use lightning to settle your problems?
Why do you make nails loosen from sheds and roofs?
Why do you do powerful damage to buildings?
Why do you begin calmly and then become a vicious rage?
Why do you use your strength to wreck ships?
Why do you make the wind blow over bins?
    Please tell me why!

James Hughes (9)
Roch Community School, Haverfordwest

Letter To A Storm

Dear Storm,
Why do you make us frightened?
Why do you roll dustbins down the road like a river?
Why are you so noisy like drums?
Why do you howl so much in the wind like a dog growling?
Why do you scare cats and dogs like a lion?
Why do you bang doors back and forth like a person running up and down the stairs?
Why do you flash so much in the sky like a torch flashing?
Why do you bang so much to wake people up
Like a cow mooing all the time?
   Please respond on the next stormy night.

Zoe Storrow (9)
Roch Community School, Haverfordwest

Letter To A Storm

Dear Storm,
Why do you roll dustbins down the road like a hamster in his hamster ball?
Why do you send lightning down to Earth to destroy all the villages and cities?
Why do you send fires to kill God's people?
Why do you slam doors back and forwards?
Why do you sound your rumble of thunder like a hippo grunting?
Why do you break lamp posts so glass scatters everywhere?
Why do you make the wind howl so much like a wolf howling madly?
Why do you make cats and dogs miaow and bark?
   Please answer my questions on the next stormy day.

Angharad Hughes (9)
Roch Community School, Haverfordwest

A Letter To The Storm

Dear Storm,
Why are you so violent when we are sleeping in our beds?
Why are you so angry and flood our streets?
Why do you roar and vibrate the ground?
Why do you flatten fences, destroy buildings works and
damage crops?
Why do you blow wind and echo?
Why do you blow a gale which makes us fall to the floor?
Why do you knock dustbins over with your mighty power?
Why do you knock down trees so we cannot drive?
　　Please write back!

Chloe Davies (10)
Roch Community School, Haverfordwest

Letter To A Storm

Dear Storm,
Why do you scare me and frighten me?
Why do you keep knocking the dustbins over in the wind?
Why do you keep sending a huge streak of lightning?
Why do you give us hailstones as hard as a rock?
Why do you howl through the windows and doors?
Why do you wreck ships and kill so many people?
Why do you growl like cats and dogs in a fight?
Why do you give us so much torrential rain?
Why do you make a dark streak across the sky?
Why are you so fierce?
　　Please respond.

Charlotte Hughes (10)
Roch Community School, Haverfordwest

Storm

Dear Storm,
Why do you get so angry and sink boats on a stormy night?
Why do you roar in the middle of the night
And try to keep me up until you get bored?
Why do you set things on fire with your flash of flickering fire?
Why do you scare our cats and dogs like someone hunting its prey?
　Please blow back.

Emil Matthews (9)
Roch Community School, Haverfordwest

My Naughty Sister Joy

My naughty sister Joy,
She annoys me all the time,
Although she's not a boy,
She takes toys of mine.

We have to share a room,
My side is very neat,
Her side is like a bomb's dropped, *boom!*
And it smells of smelly feet!

Joy has a cheeky giggle,
It sometimes starts to annoy,
She dances with a funny wiggle,
But my sister really is a joy.

Nia Lavis (9)
St Aidan's VA Primary School, Haverfordwest

My Jewel Box

If I had a velvet jewel box
Here's what I'd put inside . . .

The sweet smell of tall daffodils
Growing tall with pride.

The soft touch of my purple blanket
Which puts me to sleep at night.

The sound of the blue tit singing
And flying like a kite.

The wonderful sight of a glamorous crystal
Sparkling in the sun.

Oh I wish I had a velvet jewel box
To put my treasures in.

Alexandra Ridge (8)
St Aidan's VA Primary School, Haverfordwest

My Jewel Box

If I had a velvet jewel box
Here's what I'd put inside . . .
The sweet smell of honeysuckle
As it grows tall with pride,
The taste of delicious sweets
That I would suck all day,
The sound of crunchy chocolate
That I will not share with him.
Oh I wish I had a velvet jewel box
To put my treasures in.

George Jenkins (9)
St Aidan's VA Primary School, Haverfordwest

My Jewel Box

If I had a velvet jewel box
Here's what I'd put inside . . .
The exquisite smell of meadow sweet
Before it's black, crumpled and dried.
The taste of my mum's unimaginable pavalova
With an appetising taste, never goes to waste.
The feel of my old teddy, Little Lion,
She has a big grin on her face.
The sight of my little kitten, Muppet play,
His ginger and white patches are so lovely to see.
The sound of lions roaring
Loudly all day long!
I wish I had a velvet jewel box
To put my treasures in.

Bethan Reynolds (9)
St Aidan's VA Primary School, Haverfordwest

My Jewel Box

If I had a velvet jewel box
Here's what I'd put inside . . .
The sweet smell of blackcurrants
Which grow in the garden outside,
The touch of my smooth silk scarf
As it warms my head,
The taste of hot chocolate
As I lay in bed,
The sound of the whi
stling wind
As it passes my house.
Oh I wish I had a velvet jewel box
To put my treasures in.

Laura Swain (9)
St Aidan's VA Primary School, Haverfordwest

My Jewel Box

If I had a velvet jewel box
Here's what I'd put inside . . .
The smell of lovely white roses
Growing in my big garden outside,
The feel of my furry soft gloves
Outside in the wintry snow,
The taste of my mum putting apple pie on the table
As she starts to clear up the plates
The sound of the summer's breeze,
So relaxing on my face.
Oh I wish I had a velvet jewel box
To put my treasure in.

Jessica Viggars (9)
St Aidan's VA Primary School, Haverfordwest

My Jewel Box

If I had a jewel box
Here's what I'd put inside . . .
The sweet smell of apple pie
With the apples that grew outside.
The feel of newborn spring lambs,
So soft and bouncy in the fields.
The sound of flutes
That the orchestra needs.
The exquisite sight of the wonderful bluebells
Before the killer weeds.
Oh how I wish I had a velvet jewel box
To put my treasures in.

Emily Jones (9)
St Aidan's VA Primary School, Haverfordwest

My Jewel Box

If I had a velvet jewel box
Here's what I'd put inside . . .
The sweet smell of honeysuckle
As it grows tall with pride.
The taste of fish and chips,
My favourite food that lives by the seaside.
The birds as they fly through the air
As they glide on their side.
The sight of my little sister
Learning how to swim in the tide.
Oh how I wish I had a velvet jewel box
To put my treasures in.

Morgana Dunwoody Kneafsey (9)
St Aidan's VA Primary School, Haverfordwest

My Jewel Box

If I had a velvet jewel box
Here's what I'd put inside . . .
The beautiful smell of meadow sweet
As it grows right outside.
The touch of my soft teddy bear,
Golden fur, silver eyes.
The taste of melted chocolate,
It's even nicer than all the pies.
The sweet singing of the garden birds
As they soar into the skies.
Oh I wish I had a velvet jewel box
To put my treasures in.

Laura Williams (8)
St Aidan's VA Primary School, Haverfordwest

My Jewel Box

If I had a velvet jewel box
Here's what I'd put inside . . .
The sweet smell of an elegant red rose
Before the petals fall and the plant has died,
The soft touch of my bedspread
As it tickles my face,
The sound of blue tits singing
When they are having a race,
The sight of the glowing stars
In the night sky,
The taste of apples cooked
In the centre of a pie.
Oh I wish I had a velvet jewel box
To put my treasures in.

Katie Ridge (9)
St Aidan's VA Primary School, Haverfordwest

My Velvet Jewel Box

If I had a velvet jewel box
Here's what I'd put inside . . .

The sweet smell of honeysuckle
As it grows tall with pride.

The feel of my jumper
As my nan knits.

The luxurious taste of apple crumble
As my mum cuts it into bits.

The sound of birds chirping
As they're flying in the wind.

The sight of the trees blowing,
Some so small they look like they've just been born.

Oh I wish I had a velvet jewel box
To put my treasures in.

Louise Wheatley (9)
St Aidan's VA Primary School, Haverfordwest

My Jewel Box

If I had a velvet jewel box
Here's what I'd put inside . . .
The soothing smell of daffodils
That grow in the beautiful outside,
The taste of Mum's home-made pizza,
Very crunchy and so full of flavour,
The sight of the great spring fields
As I play with my dog eating a Quaver,
The silky touch of my long hair.
Oh I wish I had a velvet jewel box
To put my *treasures* in.

Ashley Rees-Paton (9)
St Aidan's VA Primary School, Haverfordwest

My Jewel Box

If I had a velvet jewel box
Here's what I'd put inside . . .
The lush smell of fish and chips
At the beautiful seaside.
The pleasant feel of my bed cover
As it keeps me warm at night.
The charming sound of the wind
Charging at each other to fight.
The cold taste of ice cream,
So very appetising.
Oh I wish I had a velvet jewel box
To put my treasures in.

Iestyn Griffiths (9)
St Aidan's VA Primary School, Haverfordwest

My Jewel Box

If I had a velvet jewel box
Here's what I'd put inside . . .
The sweet smell of lavender
Growing elegantly outside,
The soft feel of my teddy bear,
The one I cuddle at night,
The wonderful view of a rainbow,
It is just a beautiful sight,
The lovely sound of birds singing,
When I hear them I always grin.
Oh I wish I had a velvet jewel box
To put my treasures in.

Ella Warner (9)
St Aidan's VA Primary School, Haverfordwest

My Velvet Jewel Box

If I had a velvet jewel box
Here's what I'd put inside . . .
The sweet scent of honeysuckle
Growing tall with pride.

The soft touch of slippery silk
Running through my toes,
The wonderful taste of Mum's apple pie
Everyone eats so it goes.

The sound of spring rain falling
As it falls on my skin.
Oh I wish I had a velvet jewel box
To put my treasures in.

Megan Phillips (9)
St Aidan's VA Primary School, Haverfordwest

My Jewel Box

If I had a velvet jewel box
Here's what I'd put inside . . .
The sweet smell of honeysuckle
As it grows tall with pride.
The feel of my soft jumper
As my nan knits.
The taste of cheesy pizza
As it finally touches my lips.
The sound of the wind blowing
As it whooshes past me.
Oh I wish I had a velvet jewel box
To put my treasures in.

Sophie Mills (9)
St Aidan's VA Primary School, Haverfordwest

My Jewel Box

If I had a velvet jewel box
Here's what I'd put inside . . .
The smell of the start of springtime
And the flowers that grow with pride.
The feel of newborn puppies
That are cuddly and very soft.
The sound of crashing waves
And the sound of mice in the loft.
The sight of newborn kittens
That jump in the messy bin.
Oh I wish I had a velvet box
To put my treasures in.

Rosanna Cale (9)
St Aidan's VA Primary School, Haverfordwest

My Jewel Box

If I had a velvet jewel box
Here's what I'd put inside . . .
The feel of cold, white snow
That shines and glows outside.
The sweet smell of honeysuckle
As it grows with pride,
The sound of tweeting blue birds
Sitting on the rock near by the tide.
The taste of melting chocolate
That is hot and ready to eat.
Oh I wish I had a velvet jewel box
To put my treasures in!

Heather Lewis (10)
St Aidan's VA Primary School, Haverfordwest

My Jewel Box

If I had a velvet jewel box
Here's what I'd put inside . . .
The sweet smell of my mum's googleberry pie
With the berries that grow outside,
The touch of my warm blanket so light on my head,
The taste of fresh chicken so meaty and chewy inside.
Oh how I wish I had a velvet jewel box
To put my treasures in.

Jordan Smith (9)
St Aidan's VA Primary School, Haverfordwest

Animals In The Jungle

The lion is in the cave sleeping,
His teeth are sharp.

The baboon is up in the tree
Beating his chest.

The hippo is under the water
Sleeping in the weeds.

The elephant is holding
A mango in his trunk.

The gorilla is picking up a log,
He is very strong.

The zebra is running in the grass,
He is white and black.

The giraffe is long in the neck,
He is eating the leaves.

The parrot is flying in the air,
He is green, red, blue and yellow.

The tiger is eating a baby lion cub,
He has got sharp teeth.

The snake is hissing,
He is dangerous.

Gethin Williams (10)
St Aidan's VA Primary School, Haverfordwest

My Jewel Box

If I had a velvet jewel box
Here's what I'd put inside . . .
The smell of melted chocolate
That fills the house like a tide,
The luscious taste of strawberry ice cream
Melting down my neck,
The lovely sight of a pirate ship
As I walk down the wooden deck,
The sound of the fire alarms
On their way to stop the burn,
The touch of a car gear stick
While we sit going round a turn.
Oh I wish I had a velvet box
To put my treasure in.

Michael Dunwoody (9)
St Aidan's VA Primary School, Haverfordwest

My Jewel Box

If I had a jewel box
Here's what I'd put inside . . .
The attractive smell of Mum's apple pie
You can smell from outside.
The feel of my baby cousin's skin,
Soft and velvety to touch.
The beautiful taste of melted chocolate,
Slippery when I munch.
The sight of the orange sunset
That covers all the space.
Oh I wish I had a velvet jewel box
To put my treasures in.

Daniel Casey (9)
St Aidan's VA Primary School, Haverfordwest

I'd Rather Be . . .

I'd rather be a tick than a tock,
I'd rather be a key than a lock,
I'd rather be a shoe than a sock,
I'd rather be a door than a knock,
I'd rather be a hand than a clock.

Ruari Williams (8)
St Aidan's VA Primary School, Haverfordwest

I'd Rather Be . . .

I'd rather be a scarf than a hat.
I'd rather be a rug than a mat.
I'd rather be a kitten than a cat.
I'd rather be standing than sat.
I'd rather be thin than fat.
I'd rather be a mouse than a rat.

David Reynolds (8)
St Aidan's VA Primary School, Haverfordwest

I'd Rather Be . . .

I'd rather be a friend than not,
I'd rather be myself than lose the plot,
I'd rather be a mother than stay in a cot,
I'd rather be eating healthy food than get my teeth rot.

Josie Lewis (8)
St Aidan's VA Primary School, Haverfordwest

I'd Rather Be . . .

I'd rather be a pen than ink.
I'd rather be blue than pink.
I'd rather be a necklace than the link.
I'd rather be clean than stink.
I'd rather be lazy than think.

Mollie Hughes (8)
St Aidan's VA Primary School, Haverfordwest

I'd Rather Be . . .

I'd rather be the sea than the sand,
I'd rather be the river than the land,
I'd rather be the clock than the hand,
I'd rather be the conductor than be in the band,
I'd rather be a wife than a husband,
I'd rather be a book than a bookstand.
All these things I'd like to be,
But I'm glad that I'm just me.

Caitlin Thompson (7)
St Aidan's VA Primary School, Haverfordwest

I'd Rather Be . . .

I'd rather be a rod than a net,
I'd rather be dry than wet,
I'd rather be wild than a pet,
I'd rather be a parachute than a jet,
I'd rather be ignored than met,
I'd rather be not allowed than let,
I'd rather give than get.

Lewis Evans (7)
St Aidan's VA Primary School, Haverfordwest

I'd Rather Be . . .

I'd rather be a baby than a cot,
I'd rather be a bug than a tot,
I'd rather be alive than shot,
I'd rather be a Dalmatian than a spot.

Amy Rees (8)
St Aidan's VA Primary School, Haverfordwest

I'd Rather Be . . .

I'd rather be normal than in a band.
I'd rather be a clock than a hand.
I'd rather be water than sand.
I'd rather be in the sea than on land.
I'd rather be silly than understand.
I'd rather do a cartwheel than a handstand.
I'd rather be pasty than tanned.
I'd rather be poor than grand.

Jessica Rees (7)
St Aidan's VA Primary School, Haverfordwest

I'd Rather Be . . .

I'd rather be an orange than a peach.
I'd rather be a sentence than a speech.
I'd rather be the sky than the beach.
I'd rather be a bird than teach.
I'd rather be soap than bleach.

Louise Davies (8)
St Aidan's VA Primary School, Haverfordwest

I'd Rather Be . . .

I'd rather be snow than hail,
I'd rather be a slug than a snail,
I'd rather be ripe than stale,
I'd rather be a train than the rail,
I'd rather be a hammer than a nail,
I'd rather be straw than a hay bale,
I'd rather be pink than pale,
I'd rather be a house than jail,
I'd rather be a finger than a toenail,
I'd rather be a fish than a whale,
I'd rather be a story than a tale.

Tessa Page-Harries (8)
St Aidan's VA Primary School, Haverfordwest

I'd Rather Be . . .

I'd rather be a horse than a donkey,
I'd rather be straight than wonky,
I'd rather be a gorilla than a monkey,
I'd rather be dull than funky.

Rory Clague (8)
St Aidan's VA Primary School, Haverfordwest

I'd Rather Be . . .

I'd rather be a house than a flat,
I'd rather be a mouse than a rat,
I'd rather be a cap than a hat,
I'd rather be a dog than a cat,
I'd rather be thin than fat.

Ben Walton (8)
St Aidan's VA Primary School, Haverfordwest

I'd Rather Be . . .

I'd rather be a conductor than a band,
I'd rather be a foot than a hand,
I'd rather be the sea than the sand,
I'd rather be roly-poly than a handstand.

Katie Adams (7)
St Aidan's VA Primary School, Haverfordwest

I'd Rather Be . . .

I'd rather be the shore than the beach.
I'd rather be a slug than the leech.
I'd rather be an apple than a peach.
I'd rather be a yell than a screech.
I'd rather be shampoo than bleach.

Liam Manwaring (8)
St Aidan's VA Primary School, Haverfordwest

I'd Rather Be . . .

I'd rather be fast than slow.
I'd rather be a finger than a toe.
I'd rather be stuck than flow.
I'd rather be a square than a row.
I'd rather be a cheetah than slow.
I'd rather be tall than low.

Sarah Bennett (8)
St Aidan's VA Primary School, Haverfordwest

Wind's Ways

I start at the gate leading into the village,
I come not to plunder, I come not to pillage,
For I am the wind with a chilly sadness,
I have no heart to fill with gladness.

I glide down some steps on into the park,
I hear a blackbird and I hear a lark,
But I am not here to listen to songs,
I am here to commit some wrongs.

An elderly woman is hunched near a tree,
Wearing a bonnet as blue as the sea,
I whip it off and send it down,
Curling and whirling to a nearby town.

A ginger cat blocks my path,
I ask her to move, she will only laugh,
So up she goes, high into the air,
I believe I gave her a terrible scare!

A young dashing gent is in front of a crowd,
Speaking and standing straight and proud,
I steal his speech from out of his hand
And fling it about all over the land.

I end at the gate leading out of the village,
I came not to plunder, I came not to pillage,
For I am the wind with a chilly sadness,
I have no heart to fill with gladness.

Josephine Maidment (11)
St Aidan's VA Primary School, Haverfordwest

I'd Rather Be . . .

I'd rather be a sock than a clock.
I'd rather be four than two.
I'd rather be Piglet than Winnie the Pooh.
I'd rather be old than new.
I'd rather be me than you.

Abigail Severn (8)
St Aidan's VA Primary School, Haverfordwest

The Food Song

Mum and Dad they cut me loose
With a carton full of apple juice,
Whipped cream and strawberry pie,
It hit me right in the eye.

One, two,
Three, four,
Now my eye is really sore,
Five, six,
Seven, eight,
Then I ate a custard cake.

Hands up,
Hands down,
Then wave them all around.

Marmalade and strawberry jam,
I hate eating tinned Spam.

Now our food song is complete,
Let's sit down and eat, eat, eat!

Ben Clague (10) & Henry Partridge (11)
St Aidan's VA Primary School, Haverfordwest

Love

Your heart starts racing,
You think you are dreaming,
Love's first kiss,
No one should give it a miss,
Lots of love,
Sent from above,
Staring at stars,
Your head's in Mars,
Valentine's Day is full of love,
With peace as a dove,
No hatred or war,
Love is for ever more.

Jessica Lewis (10)
St Aidan's VA Primary School, Haverfordwest

Missing

I watch all day and watch all night,
But my pony stays out of sight.
My chestnut, fourteen two,
Has only left a brand new shoe.
My pony's mane and tail are white,
But can't be seen in the dark night.
For so long he has been gone
And never ever for so long.

At last I saw him one cold night,
His eyes glistened in the bright.
My chestnut cob, fourteen two,
Has come back to his new shoe.
My pony's mane and tail are white
And can be seen in the dark night.
For so long he has been gone
And never ever for so long.

Stephanie Ridge (10)
St Aidan's VA Primary School, Haverfordwest

Stars, Stars . . .

Glittery, glittery stars in the dark night,
Glittery, glittery stars shining white.

Sparkly, sparkly stars glowingly light,
Sparkly, sparkly stars shimmering bright.

Silvery, silvery stars shockingly clear,
Silvery, silvery stars shockingly near.

When we say goodbye to the moon,
Let's hum this little tune!

Sophie Ellis (11)
St Aidan's VA Primary School, Haverfordwest

My Pony Cariad

Cariad is funny,
I think she's a honey.
Cariad is very young,
She has a very long and furry tongue.
She's just a girl,
Often in a whirl.
She's sometimes greedy
Yet always speedy.
She's got a blaze of white,
She shines in the light.
When I lead her round
She looks at the ground.
She loudly cooed
When she was shoed.
When she's very quick
I feel too sick.
She's a mare
And I love her so dear.
This is my pony.

Alice Bennett (10)
St Aidan's VA Primary School, Haverfordwest

My Firework Poem

Sparkling fireworks
Banging and swirling
All around me.
A boom sound
Shaking the ground.
Shiny, glittering fireworks.

Sizzling fireworks crackling
In the sky, then comes the
Rockets booming in the sky.
Shiny, glittering fireworks.

Michaela Protheroe (10)
St Aidan's VA Primary School, Haverfordwest

Big Bear

I once went to the fair
And there was a big bear,
All the people there
Didn't even care.
I gave him a big pear
And he gobbled me up
And no one cared
And then he spat me out
And no one cared.
I went to the bear
And said, 'What's your name?'
'My name is Tim
And I live in bin
Made out of tin.'

Johnathon Stowell (9)
St Aidan's VA Primary School, Haverfordwest

The Bear

One day I saw a bear
And he was sitting in my chair.
I didn't know what to do
So I went to the loo
And found a sweet and started to chew.

Oh my gosh what shall I do?
I've got to get out of the loo
So I can get that bear
Out of my chair.

I went to him
And his name was Tim.
I gave him a pear,
He gobbled me down
And nobody seemed to care.

Thomas Evans (10)
St Aidan's VA Primary School, Haverfordwest

Wales

Wales might be small,
But it's a lot taller
Than you think.

The hills make it higher,
So it's more of a tire
To walk.

The sheep will bleat
You to sleep,
When you're up on the hills
At night.

Down below in the
Sleet and snow,
Everyone is happy
And proud.

They are so happy
Because their
Country is so mighty
And sound.
They might be small
But they will be tall
In their beloved *Wales!*

William Squire (10)
St Aidan's VA Primary School, Haverfordwest

My Dog Fluffy

My dog Fluffy had a big black coat.
My dog Fluffy sailed on a big black boat,
He jumped into the water and got very wet,
Then he turned into my very special pet.

Jake Griffiths (7)
St Mary's RC Primary School, Pembroke Dock

Ginger My Pet Rabbit

Ginger, Ginger
In the warm falling rain,
Sleeping out in the rain all day
With his ears flat on his back.
Ginger, Ginger
Eating Wotsits and Skips,
Sleeping with lots of crisps
In my garden's dark mist.
Ginger, Ginger
I'm here now,
You don't have to be so scared now,
Have a little rest,
You really are the best,
When you make a little racket
On a cheesy crisp packet.

Rebecca Bradley (8)
St Mary's RC Primary School, Pembroke Dock

Owls Swoop At Night

Owls swoop in their little loops at night
And sometimes give you a horrid fright
Swooping their loops at night.
Their feathers are brown and fluffy,
Helping their silent flight,
When they swoop and frighten the mice you like.
But owls say,
'We're right when we're out at night
To give those nice mice a fright!'

Joseph McElroy (8)
St Mary's RC Primary School, Pembroke Dock

Colours

Blue, blue, blue
The colour of the crashing waves.
Yellow, yellow, yellow
The colour of the setting sun.
Red, red, red
The colour of the planet Mars.
Orange, orange, orange
The colour of a juicy orange.
Green, green, green
The colour of the soft, long grass.
Black, black, black
The colour of shiny deep coal.
Brown, brown, brown
The colour of Pembrokeshire mud.
White, white, white
The colour of the nice day clouds.
Silver, silver, silver
The colour of the beautiful moon.

Emma Wilson (7)
St Mary's RC Primary School, Pembroke Dock

My Pet Cat

My pet cat,
He is black, brown and fat.
He is my buddy.
He is very funny.
Sooty sits on my dad's lap,
He likes to eat and have a nap.

Christine Sassone (7)
St Mary's RC Primary School, Pembroke Dock

Animal Alphabet

Andy is a little active ant.
Ben is a beautiful blue bird.
Carys and Caitlin are clever cute cats.
Dean is a dumb, dozy dog.
Elizabeth is a clumsy, eager elephant.
Fiona is a pink fussy flamingo.
George is a good gorgeous goldfish.
Henry is a kicking hungry horse.
Izzy is a small iguana.
Joanna is a black jolly jaguar.
Kirsty is a big kangaroo.
Leanne is a lovely lucky leopard.
Martin is a musical minded monkey.
Nick is a naughty, nasty newt.
Olivia is a slimy, slithery octopus.
Peter is a purple panting panther.
Quinn is a quivering quail.
Rhiannon is a white running rabbit.
Sophie is a slithering smiling snake.
Thomas is a turn-up turtle.
Unis is an untidy unicorn.
Victor is a vicious viper.
Walter is a massive wallowing whale.
Xavier X-rays things.
Yolande is a yelling yak.
Zena is a stripy zebra!

Sophie Harris (9)
St Mary's RC Primary School, Pembroke Dock

Animals

Owls are really nice,
Owls are big and elegant
With their yellow eyes,
Deep, deep inside they are very wise.

Tigers are very fierce,
Tigers chase deer
Day and night,
When they catch them
They feast on the meat inside.

Mice make my mum scream and shout,
My mum is afraid of them,
But deep inside
The mice are much more scared!

Rabbits skip and hop,
Wildly jumping off the ground.
Deep inside their cages
They wish to be free.

Joseph Harris (8)
St Mary's RC Primary School, Pembroke Dock

Beauty

Beauty loves me,
She loves to play
And see the sea.
She has fun
And fetches the stick.
She plays in the waves.
Beauty had pretty puppies,
We gave them away.
We were sad to say goodbye.
All the dogs are happy now.

Amy Brown (9)
St Mary's RC Primary School, Pembroke Dock

Dolphins

D ipping and diving in the deep blue sea,
O nly one dolphin all lonely,
L ovely smooth skin all shining blue,
P layful and joyful dancing the seas,
H appy and hopeful, clever and funny,
I ntelligent creatures swimming with me,
N o poacher will catch me I'm free!
S wimming and diving that's the dolphin for me.

Leanne Groves (9)
St Mary's RC Primary School, Pembroke Dock

My Dog Scruffy

My dog Scruffy is quite thin.
My dog Scruffy looks so much like a greyhound.
My dog Scruffy is fun.
My dog Scruffy is simply the best.
My dog Scruffy is scared of people he doesn't know.
My dog Scruffy was bought from a farm.
My dog Scruffy plays all day.
My dog Scruffy is a great friend.
I would not want to be without him.

Ben Thomas (9)
St Mary's RC Primary School, Pembroke Dock

Untitled

There was a young lady from Hamletti,
She ate a big bowl of spaghetti;
The spaghetti was long,
All the way from Hong Kong
And some of it got ate by the Yeti.

Laura Fursse (9)
St Oswald's VA School, Kilgetty

Do You Deserve It?

Are you bullied?
Are you hurt?
Do you deserve it? . . . *No.*
Is someone saying they're just having fun
When really they're making you run,
Run far and wide because you're scared,
Scared of hurt,
Scared of torture,
Scared of it never ending?
Are you bullied?
Are you hurt?
Do you deserve it? . . . *No.*
Have you stopped it?
Has it been and gone?
Did you tell someone? *Yes!*
That's how you stop it,
That's how it goes,
You've got to tell someone,
Anyone will do!
Have you been bullied?
Have you been hurt?
Did you deserve it?
No!

Anna Lewis (11)
St Oswald's VA School, Kilgetty

My Favourite Things

Bright late mornings,
A nice chocolate chip cookie,
The sound of seals in the sea,
Playing chase with my class,
Doing silly stuff,
The smell of Sunday roast
That soon will be on the table.

Matthew Lewis (10)
St Oswald's VA School, Kilgetty

Bullies

They know how to hurt you,
They know how to scare you,
They hurt your feelings and make you sad,
They think they're cool and they treat you like nothing.
They are very nasty,
We think they are ghastly,
They hit you,
They kick you.
Do they call you names?
If they have call a teacher and tell your mum,
Don't let it drag you away.

Richard Shaw (10)
St Oswald's VA School, Kilgetty

My Favourite Things

I like horses galloping free,
I like puppies playing on my knee.
I like kittens rolling about,
I like dolphins swimming.

I like the beach, the sand and the sea,
I like the shells shining in the sun.

I like chocolates, popcorn and sweets,
I like snow, snowboarding and skiing.
I like my friends, we all have fun
In the sun.

Emily Tranter (10)
St Oswald's VA School, Kilgetty

Bullies

Bullies are careless,
They only think of themselves,
They don't have friends,
Only make-believe.
The only thing they're good at
Is bullying and showing off.

I'd hate to be a bully,
All they do is torture,
They are very nasty
And they smell like Cornish pasty
And are very ghastly.

Bullies are rough,
Bullies are tough
And are very nasty,
Although they're not very clean.

David Colquhoun (10)
St Oswald's VA School, Kilgetty

Super Bike

S peeding through the park
U ncertain to go up the ramp
P edalling as fast as he could
E xactly in the middle
R ight, about to go up when

B oom, the bike flew into a brick wall
I njuring himself as he got up,
K een to get back on his bike
E very bone in his body ached.

Luke Hicks (10)
Sageston CP School, Nr Tenby

Birds

Birds come in all different colours like blue, red, black and green.
They have different names like blue tit, green finch, crows,
robins and magpies.
If you see some blue tits, you will be in for a surprise.
In the winter, you won't see them because they go to the west.
In the summer you may see them in the forest or in the gardens.
You can get different birds like parrots,
Some are big, some are small and some are furry.

Jessica Clarke (10)
Sageston CP School, Nr Tenby

My School Playtime

Charlie's playing around,
Tony's not making a sound.
Oh look what Georgia Thomas has found,
Sophie's spending a pound and
Beth is skipping around.
Oh no, Elle's got a pain
Luke and Dominic are stuffing shoes down the drain.
James is playing football - *Yes!* He's scored a goal,
Oliver's on a train, pretending he's getting coal.
Melissa's playing with make-up, Georgia Lewis joins in.
Oh no Gareth! Watch out you're going to sit on a pin!
Robert and Rory are searching through the bin.
Rebecca's like a shrimp jumping out of a tin.
Shannon and Rachel shout, 'It's time to come in!'
Andrew and Jessica Clarke start to sing.
Wesley's pretending he's a king
Angharad and Jessica Thomas ride their ponies round and round
All these things and more, happen each day as we all play
on each exciting and boring old school day!

Beth Jackson (10)
Sageston CP School, Nr Tenby

Summer

Summer is very hot
It's the hottest season you can get
You wouldn't want to wear warm clothes
It's too hot
It's too hot
You could go on the beach
And dive into the sea.
To see a gold coin in a clam
You rise to the surface
And smell the sweet air
You start looking for things
And see a crab with a gold coin
You take it off him and inspect it.

Rebecca Mills (9)
Sageston CP School, Nr Tenby

Running Rabbit

R unning fast across the field,
U sing all his might,
N ow and then it stops to check,
N ot knowing that it's night.
I t likes to run in the dark,
N ipping at the grass,
G oing through the trees and scratching at the bark!

R abbit run to your hole
A nd snuggle up till dusk is dawn.
B unny, scurry
B unny, hurry and hop to your goal
I t is almost time to go again
T ill dark becomes light!

Melissa Wilson (10)
Sageston CP School, Nr Tenby

Under The Sea

U nder the sea looks cold and blue
N otice the shrimps retreat quickly to a rock.
D elicious mussels hanging around,
E ach bubble of air makes it look pretty
R ocky mountains of seashells.

T he crabs disappear in the wink of an eye,
H igh ruins of Atlantis,
E very time you're under the sea, you're visiting a different world.

S lippery sea snakes wandering round the ocean blue.
E ach fish with a different face
A fter you finished, you swivel and push up to the fresh air
                                of the human world.

Gareth Folder (9)
Sageston CP School, Nr Tenby

In The Jungle

We put on our hats
Walking to the jungle
The monkey's nests are like mats
The vines are like human hair dangling down
Wales is so cold, but here it's boiling!
I told my mate let's go away
He said, 'Let's go today!'
So we went away . . .
Hip hip hooray!

Wesley Hugh Bonser (10)
Sageston CP School, Nr Tenby

My Visit To The Skate Park

I put on my pads and down I plunge,
The wind rippling my shirt
As I speed down the curvy ramp;
If I fall it'll really hurt.
As I watch my friends cheering me on,
I really hope I can roll up one side
And transfer over to the other.

Then I stop - 'Hey!' they say,
'I bet you can't go all the way round the full pipe?'
So I speed up, trembling on my board.
Now I'm at the top
Bang! 'Owww!' I hit the ground.

I pick myself up, dust myself down
And start again.
My friends gasp,
But I won't give in . . . I'm off!
Hurtling upside down at full speed,
I hear a cheer and know I've done it!

Rory Wynne-Owen (9)
Sageston CP School, Nr Tenby

The Enchanted Pet

Gracefully cantering, a steady stride
Splashes freely through the tide
Over fences, the crowd gasp!
Lots of applauding hands like
Clams opening and closing, amongst the pike.
Dressage steps so gentle and quiet.
Day ends
Horses . . . what a wonderful pet.

Georgia Lewis (10)
Sageston CP School, Nr Tenby

Galloping Horses

Gracefully cantering
Around the woods
Long legs
Long tail
On the horse
Pony! He's called
In the green field
Now they're running
Galloping into the sunset
Hay yummy, they like to eat
On the soft green grass
Racing on the track
Soft and silly mane they have
Elegant creatures
Slowing down to a trot.

Jessica Thomas (10)
Sageston CP School, Nr Tenby

The Jungle

T he lions pounding through the grass,
H ere they are as I pass,
E ven though I'm their prey.

J ungle animals are here to stay,
U nder the trees animals eat.
N ibbling grass, they rest their feet.
G obbling gorillas eat their catch.
L eaping from the big tall trees
E very animal loves their treats.

Charlotte O'Rourke (10)
Sageston CP School, Nr Tenby

Scouring Squirrels

S quirrels like hunting for nuts
C rouching when danger comes,
O utside the squirrels are very hot,
U nder their feet are very cold.
R eally hot on the squirrel's head
I 'm running up the tree.
N uts are very nice,
G reen nuts are very nice.

S quirrels are very soft,
Q uickly the squirrels run.
U nder the tree is very cosy,
I nside the tree is very warm.
R unning is very good for squirrels,
R unning up and down the tree.
E very spring the squirrels get some nuts.
L ovely, crunchy nuts.
S ome nuts are very juicy.

Rachael Robbins (9)
Sageston CP School, Nr Tenby

Scholes

S uper Scholes, he scores goals
C rossing the ball, it flies so high
H e heads it away, what a great save.
O Shea is his teammate and together they're great
L oads of songs are sung about him
E verybody loves him, nobody hates him
S choles is super, Scholes he's great.

James Hinchliffe (9)
Sageston CP School, Nr Tenby

My Favourite Things

Sweets in all different shiny bright colours
Red, blue, purple, orange and yellow
And of course gold like a full chest.
Pirates galore, fierce and strong
With swords as mighty as gods.
007 the best shot in town,
Llanelli Scarlet's the best rugby team
Dressed in a really bright red.
Poems, rhymes, funny ones too.
Acrostic, senses, shape but this type's the best of all
Chocolate:
Dark, milk and white.
I love them all
Toblerone, Terry's and Dairy Milk.
These are a few of my favourite things.

Oliver Cole (9)
Sageston CP School, Nr Tenby

Astronauts

A stronauts lolling in outer space
S illy aliens looking around
T ank of oxygen on my back
N o life on this planet
O dd aliens hovering around
N othing will stop us exploring
A liens everywhere
U ranus I can see in the distance
T reading carefully all around
S pace is a fantastic place.

Angharad Arnold (9)
Sageston CP School, Nr Tenby

The Wildlife Game

You can hear the monkeys swinging
You can feel the elephants running
You are standing under a black shadow tree.
You can feel the wind flowing in your hair,
In the distance you can see the snow melting.
You eat a banana from the banana tree,
You don't know where to go, so a monkey
Shows you around the jungle
Then you see a river
You have a drink
You get dizzy, you walk, side by side.
You feel sleepy but you have to go around the jungle.
You see trees meeting each other,
The path goes to a point and
Which way would you like to go?
Left or right?
You pick left
You want to go to the crocodile pit.
A crocodile creeping up, dragging his stomach.
You climb up a rocky hill
Your eyes start to itch.
You rub them hard
They open - it was only a dream.

Elle Joyce (10)
Sageston CP School, Nr Tenby

Under Dirty Sea

U nder the dirty and runny sea,
N ow see the runny blood from the rock.
D own below the sand, shining prize of gold,
E ating bugs in the sand
R unning fishes, going home.

D irty sand weaves into the sea,
I n the salty sea is a shark.
R usty ships on the beach
T iny shells and the fingers of the sea.
Y ou win, and tremble as you look at the ship.

S ee the birds through the waves on the sea,
E at the fish, they taste funny.
A wonderful journey!

Robert Davenport (9)
Sageston CP School, Nr Tenby

Guy Fawkes Night

It smells like toffee apples
Straight from the pocket.
It tastes like burgers sizzling
On the barbecue.
It sounds like rockets
Exploding in the air.
It feels like excitement
Flowing through my veins
It looks like jewels exploding in the air.

Dominic Hicks (9)
Sageston CP School, Nr Tenby

The Haunted House

A cry of help

S cary ghost, scary people
C ry of help in the house
A s scary as a ghost
R ain and thunder and lightning
Y ou are a very, very scary teacher.

G hosts are sometimes scary and nasty
H urry out of the haunted house
O h, angry ghost going to scare me out of my house
S orry it scared you
T errified, like Christ Watkins.

George Coles (11)
Stepaside CP School, Kilgetty

The Haunted House

Haunted houses are dark and creepy
And every night you hear screams from inside
Unknown creatures live within
No one knows what they are
The people who own it are phantoms
And every night and every day
They come to haunt and scare
How they changed, no one knows
On every full moon, you hear rattles of chains
Under the house is the dungeon
Said to contain skeletons
Of everyone who enters the house.

Adam Beynon (11)
Stepaside CP School, Kilgetty

The Haunted House On The Creepy Cliff

Beware the haunted house on the cliff,
Some people think it's real and some think it's a myth.

The Johnston people bought the house,
The creeping down the cellar door
Was it a ghost or a mouse?
The screaming got louder, more and more.

Unlucky for the mother, it was a mouse,
It wasn't just a mouse but a ghost in the house.
The children came down to eat and dine,
They had turkey and it was simply fine.

The ghost was coming for the children,
He must have thought they had a cauldron,
The Johnstons had a black cat.
You wouldn't believe how the cat was so fat.

Beware the haunted house on the cliff,
Some people think it's real and some think it's a myth.

The moans and the groans . . .
They couldn't take it any more.
Even creepier tones
Were coming from the cellar door.

When suddenly they saw the ghost.
At first he was deadly,
It went through him when he ate toast,
Then the children discovered he was friendly.

They chatted to the ghost for a while,
The mother and father thought it was simply vile.
'Do you live down the cellar door?'
'Yes I do, before I died, I swam from shore.'

Beware, the haunted house on the hill,
Some people think it's real and some think it's a myth.

James Hughes (11)
Stepaside CP School, Kilgetty

Pirates

P irates are watching, sailing through the sea.
I f they find you they will take what you have.
R aid your ship, they will kill your crew.
A fterwards you would probably end up on a desert island.
T heir black-boned cross skeleton waving out at sea.
E verybody runs as they burn down villages.
S o as the sun goes down, their true self comes out.

Cai Harris (10)
Stepaside CP School, Kilgetty

The Haunted House

The haunted house on the hill
Midnight strikes
Everything standing still.

Rattling chains
Creaking doors
The sharp werewolf's paws.

Shrieks of fear
Zombies gather
Death is near.

A ghostly mist
Bats fly
Monsters do exist.

I wake up wailing
Sweating with fear
The dream was failing.

The haunted house on the hill
Midnight strikes
Everything standing still.

Daniel Richards (11)
Stepaside CP School, Kilgetty

The Haunted House On The Hill

The ghostly house at the top of the hill,
Scary, whooshy. Calm and still.

The laughter of a ghost
That I can hear,
Delivering the post
Without any fear.

I hear the staircase creeping,
Something's by the wall,
Something big, I see it now,
It is very, very tall.

It's big and fat - not slim,
I hear a *whooshing* sound,
I cannot see it any more,
It's going round and round.

Suddenly I hear the vacuum,
It's coming near and near,
I can't get away, I've got to stay
And face my biggest fear.

The ghostly house at the top of the hill,
Scary, whooshy. Calm and still.

Kelsie Ormond (10)
Stepaside CP School, Kilgetty

The Creepy Mansion

The creepy mansion filled with fear.
The clanking, rattling in the pits down in the torture cellar.
Beware the fire-breathing dragon you might lose your hair.
But don't forget the man on the stairs.
Don't go in the armoury beneath the stairs.
Beware the coat of arms stand in pairs.
Making the hairs on your neck stand on end.
Watching your back.
I ran outside and with a fright I got in a fight.

Steven Brenchley (10)
Stepaside CP School, Kilgetty

Mr Lankershock

Mr Lankershock was sitting eating
his food when a ghost came out of nowhere
and said, '*I'm going to kill you.*'
Then the ghost vanished,
having another one of his brilliant ideas.

Then the house rocked up and down,
it was the power of the phantom of the mansion.
He made the pans and pots attack Mr Lankershock.
The scissors cut up his expensive pictures.

The parrot started going mad
and broke nearly everything in the house.
And the ghost started playing the scariest song ever
and kept on reciting, 'I am going to kill . . . *you*.'

And turned all the lights off and then someone screamed
but no one found out who it was,
or if they did, the only thing we know
is that one of them escaped and no one will know
because Mr Lankershock would have died
wouldn't he . . . ?

James Griffiths (10)
Stepaside CP School, Kilgetty

Something Strange

There once was a ghost that was so annoying,
Destroying everybody's life.
Then one day when I woke up
Everything had changed.
Lights were on,
Television was on,
The radio was even on.
So I suggested that I had to do something,
So I started to clean the house.
It was like having a spring clean
And suddenly when I was cleaning,
I *whooshed* the ghost down the plug hole.

Codie Jenkins (11)
Stepaside CP School, Kilgetty

In The Lava

Under the volcano, in the lava,
There is a creepy ghost called Marver.
He did live to thirty-seven,
And came for a ghost in Heaven.
He wasn't a person, he was a whale,
And he also looked very pale.
In the lava there is lots of mist,
But he killed millions on his list.
First it was Barbara, Marilyn and Sally,
Then it was Robert, Norman and Barry.
He only went there to say a nice prayer,
But his plan went like a dare.
On the floor was a dead body,
And the door was quite shoddy.
That is what happens when your name is Marver
And you live in boiling hot lava.

Grace Bevan (10)
Stepaside CP School, Kilgetty

Who's There?

I hear voices under my bed
They whisper, 'Beware'
And they're not the voices in my head,
I check everywhere
But nothing is there
'Help, help!' I scream.

I look in the mirror, I am so pale
I see the ghosts so I give a big wail,
They are in white cloaks and covered in chains
I panic so much, so I ask them their names.

I ask them where they are from
They say, 'We were in an explosion of a bomb,
That's why we are so white,
But we only come out at the strike of midnight.'

They ask, 'What happened to you?'
'What do you mean? I'm still alive, *boo!*'
'You don't scare us,
We're as strong as a bus.'

Lara Craig (10)
Stepaside CP School, Kilgetty

The Creepy Ghost

The moon shining on the haunted house
When I went inside I couldn't hear a mouse.
I came to the first room up the stairs
If I get eaten nobody would care.

The candlelight glowing in the dark.
I looked out the window and saw a park.
When I turned around I saw a ghost.
I think I was scared the most.

I ran into the wall
I ended up in the hall.
The ghost looked like a post
So do most.

The ghost fell down a hole
It looked like it was a mole
I'll never see him again
Until *next weekend!*

Owain Evans (10)
Stepaside CP School, Kilgetty

The Haunted House

The spooky ghost with rattling chains
He was moaning and wailing at the dot of 12 o'clock.
You can hear the tapping as it rains
On the skylight above.

There's a phantom in the cellar *beware, beware!*
He's lying in a coffin.
If you look around there are signs everywhere
To lead you to the cellar.

When you're walking past the clock
You can hear it go *ding-dong*.
Then you hear him shut the door
He slams it with a lock.

When you're walking up the stair
You see him by the wall
You can't help but stop and stare
And he disappears forever!

Rhys Bates (10)
Stepaside CP School, Kilgetty

Phantom

P hantom moves through the store.
H iding away from the owner.
A lways comes at night.
N ot very nice.
T ouching, throwing, smashing
O ver the floor.
M ysteriously disappears at daybreak.

Sam Page (11)
Stepaside CP School, Kilgetty

Beware! Beware!

Did you see the creepy house?
Beware, beware!
Rattling and smashing
Beware, beware!

Beware the ghost that comes out at night
He's coming! He's coming!
The phantom comes to haunt you.

Did you know he's real?
He's coming to get you
If you think he's not real
So beware, beware of him.

He is a ghost
So run, so run!
The smashing when you go to
The house.

Stephen Harris (10)
Stepaside CP School, Kilgetty

The Birds

B lue tits fly in the sky
I ndicating, we don't know why
R acing in the sky at risk
D ancing through the clouds
S inging lovely songs.

Richie Elliott & Carwyn Pugh
Trecastle CP School, Brecon

Birds

Birds in the sky can fly
Racing across the sky
Diving down for their feast.

In the darkness the owl flies
Night is here, owls are out hunting.

The eagle is watching, beware!
Hovering for one moment, eyes are hunting.

Starlings dance across the sky
Killers are out.

Yellow canary wants to get out, trapped in his cage
Wanting to join the others, free in the sky.

Lowri Davies (9) & Caerwyn Davies (8)
Trecastle CP School, Brecon

Eagle Poem

His claws are as sharp as blades.
He glides like a cloud upon his prey.
He stands on his mountain edge
And he swoops down like a bullet.
There he glides off into the long distance.
There he stands upon a rock, as fierce as a lion,
As brave as a man.

Moses Hart & Jorden Davies (10)
Trecastle CP School, Brecon

Birds

B uzzards blast like a rocket in the sky
I wonder how they fly?
R obin's breast is blood-red.
D oes a blue tit go high when it glides through the city sky?
S o how does it fly?

Christabel Davies (10) & Sonny Annear (8)
Trecastle CP School, Brecon

Mrs Bowen And Mr T

Mrs Bowen is as bright as the sunshine.
She is as green as ivy.
Mrs Bowen is the morning sky.
She is my teacher.

Mr T is as strict as God.
He goes as red as blood.
Mr T is as tough as Scot Gibbs.
He is my head teacher.

Jamie Bourne (10)
Trecastle CP School, Brecon

Dingo The Dolphin

She's a baby dolphin
She has slippery, slimy skin,
Her name is Dingo
And likes to eat tuna fish.

She's very friendly
But small,
She would play nice
And happy all day.

She likes to swim
With her mother,
She'll flap her flippers
The same time as her father.

When winter comes
She gets tired and bored
To swim and do tricks,
So she sleeps all day.

Natalie Jones (9)
Ysgol Carreg Hirfaen, Lampeter

My School

My school is nice
Made out of brick,
You'll get into trouble
If you're not quick.

The classroom has tables
The classroom has books,
School dinners are tasty
Prepared by two cooks.

Different sounds are heard
On the school yard,
Shouting, screaming, giggling,
Laughing, screeching and clicking.

Some teachers smell
Some teachers smile,
Some teachers are fat
And some are thin.

Melissa Carne (10)
Ysgol Carreg Hirfaen, Lampeter

My Horse

My horse is called Black Beauty,
She is a bit mad,
She is very cuddly,
Her best friend is Dad.

She is kept in a shed,
With hay and feed,
A nice cosy bed,
She's very warm indeed.

Her favourite game
Is cantering and trotting,
Her tail and silky mane,
In the wind, flowing.

Carwen Richards (9)
Ysgol Carreg Hirfaen, Lampeter

Farming

Early morning milking
just before the dawn
the cattle start lowing
while I start to yawn.

Crops are growing
Then I bale
The weather changes suddenly
I cry, 'Oh no! It's hail!'

Shearing sheep, dosing cows
Baling hay and mucking out
This is a farmer's life
Day in, day out.

John Stacey Lewis (10)
Ysgol Carreg Hirfaen, Lampeter

My Horse Flax

My horse Flax
Has a beautiful coat
Plays with Topper
In the moat.

Flax likes carrots
Every day
Doesn't like you putting
Them in her way.

I ride Flax
In the field
She bucked me off
But now I'm healed.

Katy Jones (9)
Ysgol Carreg Hirfaen, Lampeter

Wild Animals

Some are wild
Others are cunning
Some are fat
Or good at running.

Some are old
Cheetahs are spotty
Some are big
Zebras are stripy.

Some are fast
Hippos are muddy
Some are small
Hippos are lazy.

Some are slow
Snakes are nasty
Some are strong
Some are slimy.

Aled Williams (10)
Ysgol Carreg Hirfaen, Lampeter

Football Players

Footballers are big,
Footballers are small,
They all try to get the ball.

Some are short,
Some are tall
And in penalties
They make a wall.

Gethin Mathias (11)
Ysgol Carreg Hirfaen, Lampeter

My Horse Puffin

My horse Puffin,
is a very fat horse,
he likes eating muffins
and he has a lot of force.

I ride Puffin
twice a day,
he eats a lot of stuffing
and does a lot of neighs.

Puffin is a small horse,
his breed is Welsh mountain,
his coat is all coarse,
I never use my cane.

Lynwen Mathias (9)
Ysgol Carreg Hirfaen, Lampeter

My Rabbits

I've got a rabbit
She's fluffy and grey
Her name is Lleucu Llwyd
And she likes to play.

I've got another rabbit
She is brown
Her name is Twts
And she doesn't like town.

Delyth Mathias (8)
Ysgol Carreg Hirfaen, Lampeter

Owen

I would like to write a poem
About a boy called Owen,
He is like no other!
He is my little brother.

He's thin and lean
He can be mean,
He will not share
He won't play fair.

He's tall and blond,
And I'll be fond
Of him forever
And ever.

I can boss him about
I can scream and shout,
I'm allowed to
Because I'm his *big* sister!

Kiri Douglas (7)
Ysgol Carreg Hirfaen, Lampeter

My Sister

My sister is funny
She smells of honey
Sometimes she is lazy
And sometimes silly
She is very noisy
But never naughty.

Lee Davies (7)
Ysgol Carreg Hirfaen, Lampeter

My Family

I'm sure that you will find,
My family are nice and kind.

My dad is boring,
He keeps on snoring.
My mum is fun,
She likes reading The Sun.

My sister is nutty,
She likes a chip butty.
My brother is strong,
But he's often wrong.

And me!
I'm wonderful and clever,
I'm beautiful and shy,
I'm extremely honest
And would never tell a lie.

Lizzie Douglas (8)
Ysgol Carreg Hirfaen, Lampeter

My School

I like school, I go every day
If it is dry we go out to play.

If it is wet we don't go out
We stay in and scream and shout.

Tegs is at the gate
In case we are late.

Sir is in the door, he is very tall
He frightens us because
We are only small.

We are all hungry by dinner time
And that's the end of my rhyme.

Michaela Chalder (9)
Ysgol Carreg Hirfaen, Lampeter

Animals

Some animals are dangerous,
Some animals are carnivorous,
Some animals are herbivorous,
Some animals are poisonous.

Slugs and snails,
Have very short tails,
The biggest tails,
Belong to whales.

Sharks have gills,
Ducks have bills,
Dolphins breathe air,
So does a bear.

Bees live in hives,
They have very short lives,
Jellyfish live in the sea,
Some sting like a bumblebee.

Craig Richards (11)
Ysgol Carreg Hirfaen, Lampeter

My Pony

Her name is Cola
She is brown and cuddly
She lives in a field
And she's very, very muddy.

She likes to go to the river
She likes to play, drink and splash
Her breed is a Welsh mountain,
And she eats hay and grass.

Bethan Williams (10)
Ysgol Carreg Hirfaen, Lampeter

Elements

Elements, elements all over the world
Let's have a look at the forces of nature.

First is the red-hot fire
As powerful as it can be.
Then there's rock - hard or soft
But some are precious.

After comes Earth
Where plants and trees grow
Bees buzzing everywhere
Collecting honey to eat.

After that comes the wind,
It can be fun or destructive.
We're almost over
Just one more to go.

That one is water,
In sea or river
It's very, very wet.
That is the end of our search.

Rowan Marshall (9)
Ysgol Carreg Hirfaen, Lampeter

Swimming

I'm very good at swimming
But I'm not so good at running.

Plunge in the pool and
Paddle away.
In the water
I'm a fish for a day.

I'll put on my goggles and jump in.
Everybody shouts
Hooray I hope you win!

Tomos Williams (8)
Ysgol Carreg Hirfaen, Lampeter

My Farmer

The farmer is old,
The farmer is cold,
Cow is milking,
Cow is calving.
Sheep is shearing,
Sheep is lambing,
A smelly shed
Is an animal bed.
Farmer has dirty clothes with holes
Farmer has string hanging from his pockets.
Farmer takes his time
Farmer has hay in his stinky old wellingtons.
Messy old farmer,
Stinky old farmer,
Greedy old farmer,
Pongy old farmer.

Dylan Watkins (10)
Ysgol Carreg Hirfaen, Lampeter

My Friend

He watches TV and he has a big tree.
He lives in a caravan and he's a Man U fan.
When he's in the crowd he shouts very loud.
If they lose he goes on a cruise.
He has a boat and he loves his coat.

Shaun Davies (8)
Ysgol Carreg Hirfaen, Lampeter

Snow

One night it was snowing
Like a blizzard dropping everywhere
Snowflakes on the gates
-6°C, it was freezing.

I went for a walk
My cheeks turned red
The wind whistled fast
Pushing me away.

Cars were battling in the blizzard
Windscreen full of ice
Lights flashing aggravating other cars
People beeping horns.

Animals shivering, no coat
Birds flying to the north
Couldn't see anything - mist everywhere
I wish it would snow every day!

Christina Davies (10)
Ysgol Carreg Hirfaen, Lampeter

Football Mad

Football can be played by people big and small.
I like to play football because it's played with a ball.
I play with all my friends, eleven on each side,
The whistle is about to blow
So now I'd better go.

Sam Jacobs (9)
Ysgol Carreg Hirfaen, Lampeter

Space

Entering the atmosphere of Mercury,
I think it's quite jerky
But isn't too perky.

Now entering the atmosphere of Venus,
It's very victorious
But also quite vicious.

Now entering Earth's atmosphere,
It's the place that gave birth
To all sorts of beasts and feasts
That inhabit the Earth.

Also entering Mars' atmosphere,
Muddy and soggy
Also known as the Red Planet.

Jupiter's atmosphere is enormous
And the fifth from the sun
It also has a red spot.

Saturn's atmosphere is round
And is like an enormous globe,
Which has eighteen moons.

Now entering Uranus' atmosphere,
Big enough to swallow the Earth 64 times,
It has a mighty magnetic force.

Neptune's atmosphere is so long
Like Neptune's year,
Its blue world mysteries await.

Entering Pluto's atmosphere,
It's the smallest in all
Of the galaxy.

Rhys Price (9)
Ysgol Carreg Hirfaen, Lampeter

My Pet

Name of my pet is Jaci Soch,
He lives in a cage with his brother,
His name is Tomos Caradog.

He has black eyes and colourful fur,
With gel in his hair,
And little sharp claws.

When I want to touch him,
He runs away like a hare
But when I catch him he's very cuddly.

When I put carrots
And new bed in his cage,
He runs to get the best spot.

He is very greedy
But he does share
With his brother.

Cerys Roberts (9)
Ysgol Carreg Hirfaen, Lampeter

The Sea

There are fish in the sea.
There are crabs in the sea.
There are lovely coral in the sea.
There are snappy, dangerous sharks in the sea.
There are whales and dolphins in the sea.
Dolphins are fast and whales are big!
But the best thing of all is yummy fish and chips
And lobster and crab to eat.

Sion Hughes (8)
Ysgol Carreg Hirfaen, Lampeter

My Friend

He has green eyes
He has brown hair,
He is quite tall
His nose is small.

He likes football
He likes swimming,
He can run fast
And is never last.

He likes to help
On his grandad's farm,
To feed the hungry sheep
And milk cows in the barn.

Steffan Roberts (8)
Ysgol Carreg Hirfaen, Lampeter

Mum

My mum is so brilliant,
She's cool and she's kind,
She loves to go shopping,
Come rain or shine.

She does all the washing,
Cooking and cleaning,
Tidies my room
And helps with my reading.

She's caring and friendly
To all that she knows.
She's a mum in a million
And I love her loads.

Beca Creamer (8)
Ysgol Carreg Hirfaen, Lampeter

Football

Football's the name
What a great game!

Sitting in front of the TV
It's a goal *yippee!*

Liverpool's the team for me
But will they win on Saturday?
We will have to wait and see.

Dafydd Williams (9)
Ysgol Carreg Hirfaen, Lampeter

My Cat

My cat is called Abby.
My cat likes to sit on mats.
My cat is a tabby.
She likes to chase rats.
My cat is very nice.
She likes to chase mice.

Dominic Lee (8)
Ysgol Carreg Hirfaen, Lampeter

My Brother

My brother keeps me awake at night
And always makes me want to fight.
He is so tall and is 11 years old
But still we want to play out in the cold.

Lloyd Richards (8)
Ysgol Carreg Hirfaen, Lampeter

Rhys

This is a boy with a smile on his face.
He always wants to win a race.
He likes to play with his bat and ball.
I'm sure he will grow up to be tall.

He thinks he's the chef and likes to bake.
He loves and enjoys Mamgu's cake.
He watches wildlife films like mad
And likes to work in the yard with his dad.

At one he was out of his nappy
When he eats sweets he's very happy.
He doesn't like a row or to be told.
But my little brother has a heart of *gold*.

Sioned Douglas (9)
Ysgol Carreg Hirfaen, Lampeter

Football

Football is played with a ball.
The aim is to kick it in the goal.

Some players will miss, some will score.
Some games will end in a draw.

The fans will shout, the fans will scream.
They'll do anything to support their team.

They sing their songs all in a rhyme.
The whistle blows, it's now full-time.

Dylan Evans (8)
Ysgol Carreg Hirfaen, Lampeter

Butterflies

Butterflies are so cool
I see them when I go to school,
I like to see them flying in the sky
I only see one at a time - I wonder why?

Lauren Gray (7)
Ysgol Carreg Hirfaen, Lampeter

Mum

My mum likes chatting on the phone
But it makes me want to moan.

She likes to cook for me,
Something nice for tea.

She often goes shopping
And her other hobby is walking.

Bethan Williams (7)
Ysgol Carreg Hirfaen, Lampeter

Rabbit

I'd love to have a pet rabbit
But Mum won't let me have it.
'It's too expensive to keep,' she said.
But I'm sure she's just very scared.

Nicola Jones (8)
Ysgol Carreg Hirfaen, Lampeter

Pets

Pets are animals, cats and dogs,
Cows and fish or smelly hogs,
Sheep that bleat and goats that eat,
Horses that eat sugarbeet,
Hamsters bite in the light,
They spin their wheel in the night,
Rabbits eat juicy carrots,
There's a type of bird called a parrot,
Some are big, some are small,
Animals we love them all!

Lowri David (9)
Ysgol Griffith Jones, St Clears

Witches

Witches, witches everywhere,
Don't go out you'll have a scare,
If you see a grizzly,
Run away, he'll eat your hair,
If you go to the fair,
You must beware,
Hope you win a teddy bear.

Wayne Broeckhoven (10)
Ysgol Griffith Jones, St Clears

Sport

Rugby is my favourite sport,
Also playing tennis on the court,
Football also is quite fun,
Getting muddy in the sun!
Running makes me very hot,
Too many sweets make my teeth rot!

Edward Noblett (9)
Ysgol Griffith Jones, St Clears

Sports

I like surfing in the sun,
Playing football can be fun,
Swimming pool I don't like much,
Runner's cross-country makes me puff!
Snowboarding is really cool,
I like playing snooker and pool,
Snowmobiles are lots of fun,
Flying past everyone.

Brandon Davies (9)
Ysgol Griffith Jones, St Clears

I Like

My tummy is rumbly
Jelly is wobbly,
Oranges are fruit,
I like Fruit Shoot.

I like sweets,
I like treats,
I like bubblegum,
So do my chums.

Jodie Stickland (9)
Ysgol Griffith Jones, St Clears

Animals

A nimals are a living thing,
N eons are a type of fish,
I nsects live underground,
M ammals have warm blood,
A nteaters eat ants,
I have a hamster called Buttercup,
S he is a little rascal.

Abbey Rees (9)
Ysgol Griffith Jones, St Clears

Why Not?

Why not have an elephant,
That's higher than the clouds?

Why not have a dog,
That barks very loud.

Why not have a monkey that
Swings tree to tree?

Why not have a cat
Maybe one or two or three?

Why not have a donkey
That sips all your drink?

Why not have a tiger
Yellow, blue or pink?

Why not feed your pet green peas,
Daisies, buttercups and green leaves?

Amy Hill (10)
Ysgol Griffith Jones, St Clears

Books!

Big books, small books,
Books everywhere,
Go to a shop,
And they'll be there.
Tiger books, some on history too,
Encyclopaedias for me and you.
Animal books, science too,
Books for me and
Books for you!

Lloyd Rees (9)
Ysgol Griffith Jones, St Clears

Being A Girl

I am such a girlie girl,
With a beaded necklace and a pearl,
All my flashy, glitzy clothes,
How many I have, no one knows?
A dining dress and flashy suits,
Not to forget the high heel boots,
Dying my hair pink and blue,
And there's still enough to share with you.
Decorating bags as you can see,
A pink flower and a busy bee,
Do you wonder why I like being me?
Well if you're a girl, you'll soon see!

Ruth Elms
Ysgol Griffith Jones, St Clears

Chocolate

Chocolate is very sweet,
Having it is a real treat,
There are lots and lots of chocolate bars,
Kit-Kat, Penguins, even Mars.
Easter eggs and chocolate dips,
Chocolate cookies with chocolate chips.
Eating all your Easter eggs and
Chocolate men with chocolate legs.
Chocolate is sweet, you all know why,
But now it's time to say goodbye!

Flora Upton (9)
Ysgol Griffith Jones, St Clears

Dreaming

My mother thinks I am in my room working,
But I am not!
I am in my flying saucer in Africa.

My father thinks I'm reading a book,
But I am not!
I am riding a hippo in the jungle.

My sister thinks I'm in the bathroom
But I am not!
I'm sunbathing in the beach.

My brother thinks I'm listening to music
But I am not!
I'm up in the sky dreaming of pop stars.

Mr Edwards I'm doing my work
But I am not!
I am flying in my chocolate saucer.

Sarah Tomlinson (9)
Ysgol Gynradd Cwmgors, Ammanford

The Buzzard

The buzzard was gliding in the sky,
With his delicate wings hooked beak
And storming yellow eyes.
He's bored day after day trying to catch prey,
Today in a fine day to hunt,
Finally he sees something,
It is a succulent juicy rabbit,
And it is his favourite food,
He's not hungry again!

Nicholas Jones (10)
Ysgol Gynradd Cwmgors, Ammanford

The Lighthouse

I like to dream of a lighthouse,
A lighthouse with no rats inside,
With no spiders and no webs,
And no dust on the lights.
I like to dream of the
Lighthouse keeper keeping
The lighthouse clean and safe.
The lighthouse keeps the boats
Safe from the rocks around it.
But I love to dream of an island,
With the lighthouse on top,
It is there to get a better look,
So then the light can shine,
To dock to dock to dock,
Two people live here,
They live in a cave,
One of them is the lighthouse keeper,
Can you guess who?

Gemma Griffiths (10)
Ysgol Gynradd Cwmgors, Ammanford

My Best Friend

My best friend is the best in the world,
She is always there for me
When I am in trouble or when I am sad or lonely,
She has nutmeg coloured hair and
Brown eyes and rosy cheeks.
She is the funniest girl I know on this planet,
And her name is Gemma Jones.

Jessica Jones (11)
Ysgol Gynradd Cwmgors, Ammanford

Daydreaming

My mother thinks I am doing homework,
But I am not
I am whirling around the moon in my brand
New rocket catching aliens.

My teacher thinks I am doing an essay,
But I am not,
I am in Wimbledon playing tennis against
Tim Henman and I have won the game.

My father thinks I am sleeping,
But I am not
I am saving the world with Spider-Man from the Green Goblin.

Mr Edwards thinks I am writing a story,
But I am not,
I am in a never before discovered land in the sea
With turtles and dolphins and whales.

Elin Angharad Halfpenny (10)
Ysgol Gynradd Cwmgors, Ammanford

My Spacecraft

I have a spacecraft which is red and blue
I look for aliens,
That is what I do,
The alien's colour is autumn gold,
Don't keep the alien too long,
Because it will turn to mould,
Sometimes if you go to space
You will find it's a big empty place.
The colour of the fire is
Grenadier red,
Don't walk through it because you will be dead.
There is not a lot to say about my spacecraft,
What can I do? Where can I go?
Please can you help?

Lewis Reddy (10)
Ysgol Gynradd Cwmgors, Ammanford

My Rocket

My rocket is big and blue,
What people say
Is what I do,
Flying high,
Through the big blue sky.

Gender red is the colour of my flame,
I'd better be careful,
So I don't catch a plane,
I use my flame for my roast,
If you go through it you will be toast.

Chasing aliens with my big blue rocket,
I'd better take it steady,
Or I'll blow my socket,
Because what people say
Is what I do.

Andrew Smith (11)
Ysgol Gynradd Cwmgors, Ammanford

My Daydream

My mother thinks I'm doing my homework
But I'm not.
I'm dreaming that I'm playing in the World Cup Final
Scoring the final goal in a penalty shoot-out to win.

Mr Edwards thinks I'm doing mental maths
But I'm not.
I'm dreaming that I'm in a rally championship
Skidding and going more than 50 miles per hour.

My father thinks I'm watching TV
But I'm not.
I'm dreaming that I'm playing rugby with the Scarlets
Against Toulouse and winning the European Cup.

My grandfather thinks I'm playing cards
But I'm not.
I am dreaming that I am an Egyptian
Looking at the mummy pharaoh, and the spooky pyramids.

Iestyn Jones (9)
Ysgol Gynradd Cwmgors, Ammanford

The Amazing Earth

Amazing Earth, the one and only
once before so lost and lonely.
But now it is lucky for it grows lots of greenery
and has beautiful mountain tops with lots of scenery.

Amazing Earth has lots of colours
like thornberry red that describes flowers.
Amazing Earth holds many fantastic treasures
not just below but above and all around us.
Amazing Earth has lots of weathers
in the sun and snow we play together.
But in horrible rainstorms and foul winds
I play a board game and hope to win.

Amazing Earth has its cruel ways
like hurricanes and earthquakes day by day.
I have really got to say
people find amazing things about Earth every day!

Alex Horanszky (10)
Ysgol Gynradd Cwmgors, Ammanford

The Falcon

At the break of day a falcon patrols the red sky
with its plumage shining like the Queen's magnificent gem stones.
On its quest to find food with its brilliant eyesight
and razor-sharp talons.
When the falcon finds its prey, it's in a rocket-like shape
and starts to plummet towards the ground
to snatch its prey from the field.
The falcon, lord of the sky,
with its feathers shining in the sun's rays.
The falcon, king of the birds and a fierce hunter.
But in May they become caring parents,
caring for the Arran white chicks in the nest.

Joseph O'Conner (10)
Ysgol Gynradd Cwmgors, Ammanford

Wishful Thinking

My mother thinks I'm doing homework
But I'm not
I'm dreaming of dancing
I'm thinking of creamy fudge chocolate
Swimming in a pool of milkshake
When servants are giving me more

My mother thinks I'm cleaning my room
But I'm not
I'm secretly talking to my friend
On my caramel-coloured phone
My bedroom's a dusty-pink colour
Like a raspberry in the sun

My father thinks I've taken the dog for a walk
But I'm not
I'm playing football with a crunchy nut egg
When my dog's barking by the tree
I'm carrying on playing with my favourite sweets.

Joanna Elliott (11)
Ysgol Gynradd Cwmgors, Ammanford

My Best Friend

My best friend has brown hair and blue eyes,
She sticks up to bullies,
She's not afraid of anything,
She's my best friend,
She never bullies anyone,
She's a gentle kind friend,
Her name is Elin.

Megan Lewis (9)
Ysgol Gynradd Cwmgors, Ammanford

Show Jumping

Cantering and galloping in the field
while people are watching and making deals.
Leaping over coloured poles,
and little boxes with wide holes.
I'm holding firmly to the reins,
and blood is rushing through my veins.

Everybody is gazing at me,
while my mother is drinking tea.
I'm ready for the next jump
and when I land I'll have a bump.
I've now completed the course
and give a pat to my horse.

The judge said, 'You've done well,
but on the last jump you fell.'
Silently I led my horse out
and I was in a bit of a pout.
I took him in the stable
and knew I wasn't able
to compete in the championship.

Brittony Price (10)
Ysgol Gynradd Cwmgors, Ammanford

My Best Friend

My best friend is nice, kind and intelligent.
She has got long brown hair and green eyes.
She's always there for you if you need something.
She has a brilliant voice and excellent dance moves.
She has got a brother and she lives with her mother and father.
My friend has got three dogs, chickens, ducks and a lot
                                          of other animals.
She has got a lot of other friends.
She never argues with anyone.
She is 11 years old and she likes horses more than anything.
The colour of her bedroom is orange and yellow like a fire colour
And her mother drew a big unicorn on her wall and coloured it in
With paint and spray.
That's Brittony.

Jade Johns (11)
Ysgol Gynradd Cwmgors, Ammanford

My Life

When I was born I had a little yawn,
    My mother didn't see me.

When I was one I said hello but
    My dad didn't hear me.

When I was six my mother nor
    My dad could catch me.

When I become sixteen I will
    Be going out dancing all the time.

When I become a mother my children
    Will drive me up the wall!

Lucy Symons (11)
Ysgol Gynradd Cwmgors, Ammanford

My Daydream

My mother thinks that I am doing my homework
    but I am not
I am dreaming that I am scoring a goal
in the premiership
while the crowd go crazy.

My father thinks that I am in my bedroom
    but I am not
I am dreaming that I am in a boat
driving through the rough sea
and winning the boat race.

My mother thinks that I am watching TV
    but I am not
I am dreaming that I am in a Mitsubishi rally car
driving through mud, zooming around corners
and having fun.

My father thinks I am sleeping
    but I am not
I am riding a motorbike
doing a front flip, overtaking everybody
and winning the super cross cup.

Rhys Williams (10)
Ysgol Gynradd Cwmgors, Ammanford

My Daydream

My mother thinks I am doing my homework
but I am really playing in the FA premier league with Man U
scoring the second goal.

My father thinks I am playing my PlayStation but I am not
I am in the road rally championship speeding around a corner.

My grandmother thinks I am baking cakes
but I am really swimming in the sea
playing with dolphins.

My auntie thinks I am playing on my bike
but I am playing a guitar with Busted.

My grandfather thinks I am sleeping
but I am in the super cross championship in Cardiff
jumping over a ramp.

My father thinks I am eating my breakfast
but I am in a rally car with Colin McRae.

My mother thinks I am on the computer
but I am really in space on the moon.

Ben Cooke (10)
Ysgol Gynradd Cwmgors, Ammanford

Butcher Boy

Butcher Boy is
A giant
He kills like a blade
He is a man-eater
Human beings get away!
He would groan if he got them
He'd make them bleed
Then feed
Leave no bones
Hunting he would go!

Richard Jones (10)
Ysgol Gynradd Wirfoddol Myfenydd, Llanrhystud

The Best Pet That I Ever Had

The best pet I ever had
Was a monstrous dog
He wasn't bad
Well, he was really
Completely mad!

His favourite menacing thing was
Destroying my great sock set
Which led me
To a terrible debt.

When the gentle postman arrived
My dog would run at him
Make him forget the post
And escape down the coast.

Jos Jones
Ysgol Gynradd Wirfoddol Myfenydd, Llanrhystud

Princess Nambia

Princess Nambia,
she's bad,
and utterly mad.
She isn't fat,
but such a rat,
what an idiot.
She has two cats
to chase all three bats.
She came,
without fame,
what a pain.

'It's not fair
please be a friend,'
she shouted sadly.
'I'm not sly
I'm just a normal guy,'
as if she's nice!

Gwenllian Rees-Evans (10)
Ysgol Gynradd Wirfoddol Myfenydd, Llanrhystud

Blood Bottler

He is big and thin.
He's a bully and a nasty beast
called the Blood Bottler.
He pushes and kicks and
calls children names.
The teachers are so scared they don't want him
to get in a temper.
They went to the gigantic chocolate factory.
The Blood Bottler climbed
up the stairs.
He stood at the enormous
bowl of choc,
and the tiniest child pushed
him over
    let him
        drown
            drown
                drown
                    drown.

Aled Davies (10)
Ysgol Gynradd Wirfoddol Myfenydd, Llanrhystud

My Dad And Mum

My dad is bossy,
I don't like it.
It is like your worst nightmare,
he is like evil Miss Snitt.

My mum is always lazy,
I do it all,
horrible, horrible, horrible,
I am only small.

My mum and dad
put together are worse.
I don't like it.
It is like a curse!

Eleanor Farley (10)
Ysgol Gynradd Wirfoddol Myfenydd, Llanrhystud

I Wish I Stayed A Bit Longer

I wish I'd stayed a bit longer
I wish I could have played
with my cousins, aunties and uncles
nearly every day.
I wish I could have stayed a bit longer
to see the world of archaeology.
I wish my first time in Indonesia
could have been a little longer.
Time to be with my family
talking to them.
Learn more about their traditions
and them learn about mine.
I wish I could have stayed a bit longer.

Edgar Bewers (9)
Ysgol Gynradd Wirfoddol Myfenydd, Llanrhystud

Scar

Scar, Scar is so mean
Kills Lion King's warriors,
Running madly in a war.
Monsters dying, left his bones.
Silly noises from Scar's friends
Scar had a scar on his head.
Lives in a cave, very spooky,
Rocks are falling on their heads.
Animals joining in the war.

Night-time starts the real match.
Scar and Lion King.
Scar gets knocked down the cliff
Groaning, moaning, 'Please help me
Help me
I'm the best pest
Noooooo!'

Sion Owen (9)
Ysgol Gynradd Wirfoddol Myfenydd, Llanrhystud

The Blood-Bottler

Hey Blood-Bottler, come over here!
Why should I, you little prawn?
Sit down, Blood-Bottler
Stop spitting when you're sitting.

Hey stop hitting me or else!
Don't make me come over there.
That's it, I've had it with you!
Ow! That hurt!
Stop it Blood-Bottler!
Help! Help! Help!

Gethin Davies (9)
Ysgol Gynradd Wirfoddol Myfenydd, Llanrhystud

Yellow

Yellow is the sun
As yellow as a banana
Yellow is a banana
As yellow as the moon
Yellow is the moon
As yellow as a candle
Yellow is a candle
As yellow as a flame
Yellow is a flame
As yellow as the sunset
Yellow is the sunset
As yellow as a buttercup
Yellow is a buttercup
As yellow as a cushion
Yellow is a cushion
As yellow as a star
Yellow is a star
As yellow as the sun.

Emma Morris (9)
Ysgol Gynradd Wirfoddol Myfenydd, Llanrhystud

The Evil Voldermort

Voldermort is so wicked
More wicked than all the rest
He has many followers
He thinks they are big pests.

'Harry Potter, you are mine!'
Voldermort said so fierce
Then he floated far into the night
He really was mysterious.

One day he came back
So very hidden
No one's allowed to say his name
Because it is forbidden.

'So we meet once again!'
He waved his magic wand
Harry P did the same,
'To kill you I have longed!'

So off they went to kill each other
Voldermort was the worst
Bang! Boom! *Fzzt!*
'Thanks to you my little friend I am now cursed!'

In the end
Everyone was freed
Voldermort was killed at last
To be scared of him, there is no need.

Gareth Lloyd (11)
Ysgol Gynradd Wirfoddol Myfenydd, Llanrhystud

What Would Happen If?

What would happen if dragons were real?
There'd be as many humans as the poor dodo.
What would happen if the sky fell?
We'd be surrounded by oversized candyfloss
That squirted water every so often.
What would happen if humans were fish?
We'd be scared of birds, not them scared of us.
What would happen if the crater-covered moon fell to Earth?
A big bowling ball would wipe out all existence.
What would happen if the dodo was still alive?
People would still hunt them and they would die.

What would happen if dragons were real . . . ?

Joey Sinclair (10)
Ysgol Gynradd Wirfoddol Myfenydd, Llanrhystud

A Little Pet

I had a little pet
That went to see the vet
I had a little cat
That lived in a hat.

The teeny-weeny pet at the vet's
Was a little dog
'A dog for a pet?'
Asked the vet
'Come and see some of these.'

I met lots of creatures
From cats to rats
Bears to bees
And kids with cheese!

I think I'll stick to my little pet!

Ffion Tansley-Furr (9)
Ysgol Gynradd Wirfoddol Myfenydd, Llanrhystud

My Crazy Cat

I had a little pet once
The best in all the world
She ran around really madly
She was the greatest of all dancers as she twirled.

My little pet was a cat you know
She was a fan of all athletics
Once she got so poorly
She had to have antibiotics.

Even though my cat was very athletic
She did adore her food
Although she was funny and so cool
She could also be quite rude.

Two nasty years ago
I lost my funky cat
She had a good sense of humour
And loved her tasty rat!

Marisa Morgan (9)
Ysgol Gynradd Wirfoddol Myfenydd, Llanrhystud

Snow

Cold, like ice,
As soft as a pillow.
I would love to be made of snow.
We never see
Snowflakes falling
From the bright, shining sky.
I wish I could catch a cold snowflake
That turned into wet water;
Make a snowman as tall as a giant,
Who would be my friend . . .
. . . Made of snow.

Ffion Evans (7)
Ysgol Gynradd Wirfoddol Myfenydd, Llanrhystud

My Tiger

The best pet that I ever had was a terrific tiger
It had a huge hump
Great stripes
And it loved to jump.

It had an orange toilet
And a herbal refresher thing
From his point of view it was fashionable
But the toilet still had a ming.

He was really cool
Played rock
On a guitar
Wearing a frock.

He loved his food
Asked for more
Slurpy spaghetti
He'd already had four.

They took him away
He really caused a row
It was all for the best
But I really miss him now.

Kathryn Botting (9)
Ysgol Gynradd Wirfoddol Myfenydd, Llanrhystud

The Best Pet That I Ever Had

Bracken was my favourite cat
Oh she was an amazing pet
Eighteen was her age
As fast as a jumbo jet.

She was a very brave cat
Slash! Slash!
She pulverised wimpy dogs
She was worth some cash.

The old shattered Bracken
Soon fell ill
She rammed a gigantic dog
And took a steroid pill.

Bracken tried her best
But in the end she died
We all loved Bracken
I simply cried and cried.

Steffan Evans (11)
Ysgol Gynradd Wirfoddol Myfenydd, Llanrhystud

A Game Of Football

The ball is a zebra
running away from a tiger.
Other players are cheetahs
trying to capture their supper.
The goalie is a salmon trying to survive.
The referee, running,
like a dolphin swimming away from a shark.
A striker heading for the goal,
like a lion abusing its prey.
Football is wild.

Jamie Tyler-Lloyd (8)
Ysgol Gynradd Wirfoddol Myfenydd, Llanrhystud

Venalicious

Venalicious is a vicious villain
The worst in all of Greece
But his mother would just say
'He really wants to make peace!'

Venalicious runs about
Like a madman
Always shouting behind you
'Run! Run! The Jackal Clan!'

His hands are as rough as a filing board
His face as black as tar
A terrifying cry he has
But he doesn't drive a car.

One ear was torn off
He is revolting and very vile
You really don't want to look at
His horrible, crooked smile.

Long matted hair
An ugly gash on his head
When he is angry
His face goes all red.

Andrew Fricker-Power (11)
Ysgol Gynradd Wirfoddol Myfenydd, Llanrhystud

Darth Vader

Darth Vader is so vile
Putrid pile of plastic
A true believer of the dark force
That once led him off course.

Darth Vader gasps and grasps
Because he is mechanical
Black
Looks like an old sack
'I'm Darth Vader, I'm a mean kid!'

Light and dark heart.

He was playing with pink Barbies one day
And the roof gave way
In falls Luke Skyfaller
With a tennis bat.

Darth Vader stood up
Gave Luke a slap
Started to bully
Luke shouted, 'Stop you scally!'

Darth Vader took no notice
Luke just shouted
'By jovey I think I've got it!'
And slapped him back.

Luke hit
A bit
Then crafty people came
From the asylum to play
And took Darth Vader away.

Steffan Woodruff (11)
Ysgol Gynradd Wirfoddol Myfenydd, Llanrhystud

I Had Seen A Little Pet

'Can we get a dog, Mum?'
I had seen a little cute dog
As cuddly as a baby hamster
Much nicer than a frog.

'Please can we have it, oh please, Mum?'
'OK, but in October.'
'Dad will let me won't he?'
I asked and he said November.

'But Dad, November is too long.'
'OK, we'll get him today.'
'And get him some toys too?
I can't wait to go home to play!'

Michaela Richards (10)
Ysgol Gynradd Wirfoddol Myfenydd, Llanrhystud

Mog

I had a little pet
It was a little slimy frog
It had a very weird name
His name was Mog.

We played around every day
We really got quite wet
We were best friends, me and Mog
But he was just my pet.

I woke up one morning
And felt him on my leg
He was so sound asleep
Oh no! He was dead!

Every day I went to school
All I could do was think of him
Now I've got a new slippery frog
His name is Tim.

Coral Kennerley (9)
Ysgol Gynradd Wirfoddol Myfenydd, Llanrhystud

I Am A Little Horse

I am a little horse
I love to play games
I like to go for rides
But I always pull on my reins.

I love to run and run
Out in the open air
But when I get back home
There's always something stuck in my hair.

My hair is really long
Nearly right down to the floor
When I go and get my food
I always want some more.

I sleep in the moonlit stable
On the nice warm hay
And if you really want to know
My name is May.

Kara Knowler-Davies (11)
Ysgol Gynradd Wirfoddol Myfenydd, Llanrhystud

The Sea

Blue, noisy and cold waves,
sometimes you can fish in it,
sometimes you can't
depending on the weather.
Once I caught a fish
but it wriggled free.
Wish I'd caught it properly
and taken it home for my supper.
The sea,
a large swimming pool,
the waves like a pair of hands, but much colder,
carrying you in its arms.
I love the sea.

Sean François (8)
Ysgol Gynradd Wirfoddol Myfenydd, Llanrhystud

The Sea

A blue trampoline reaching across,
touching the sky.
Its waves are like a tree growing up high,
from its sandy roots to its watery leaves.
A blue friend, always there for you
when it is happy and calm,
but a great enemy too,
it is a tough and ferocious boxer in its anger.
But the sea is my friend.

Rhys Nicholls (9)
Ysgol Gynradd Wirfoddol Myfenydd, Llanrhystud

Spider

I am a little spider
All nice and hairy
No one likes me
They all think I'm scary.

Well at least I have one friend
Sam, he is my mate
But then someone else will come, someone like
Kate!

Kate will try to kill me
But then Sam will say
'No, don't kill him'
And then it will be okay.

Kate is a mean little girl
That hates animals
You never know what she'll do to yours
She is a cannibal!

Anwen Flynn (10)
Ysgol Gynradd Wirfoddol Myfenydd, Llanrhystud

My Invisible Friend

My sporty friend is invisible.
He is the bestest friend
anyone can have.

When I'm crying
he wipes my tears.
He comes to my house
when I am lonely.
He shares my jokes,
he makes me laugh.

We play football together,
he is not a skilful striker
like Michael Owen,
or a fast passer like Ryan Giggs,
or a diving goalie like Tim Howard.
But he is good company,
he is my best friend.

Carys Evans (8)
Ysgol Gynradd Wirfoddol Myfenydd, Llanrhystud

My Lover Boy

My lover boy is sweet,
kind and helpful.
I love him because he is honest
all the time.
I loved my lover boy,
until he fell in love with another girl.
I wish I had never fallen in love,
even though he was not real,
my dream lover boy.

Charlotte Robinson (9)
Ysgol Gynradd Wirfoddol Myfenydd, Llanrhystud

The Good And The Bad

People,
some are good, some are bad.
Good people
are helpful and kind,
honest like my uncle.
Sharing things like sweets.
Nice, caring people.

Bad people
smash windows and keep guns,
get chased by the police,
most of them get away with it
but naughty people should beware!

Nobody knows why people do bad things
especially the good.

Louis Langford (8)
Ysgol Gynradd Wirfoddol Myfenydd, Llanrhystud

My Cat

Felix, my cat,
Follows me around like a little star,
Fluffy and cute,
Not as wild as a tiger,
Felix, my cat,
Miaow! Miaow!

Heidi Hughes (8)
Ysgol Gynradd Wirfoddol Myfenydd, Llanrhystud

The Haunted Castle

One spooky, dark night
in the eerie haunted castle
lived an old, crinkly, crooked witch.
She cackled as she made smelly potions
and sneakily gave people poisonous apples
to ruin the world.
One spooky, dark night the witch had a visitor,
he had a gun!
'Hands up,' he said.
'We know what you've been doing!'
And that was the end
of the crinkly, crooked witch
in the eerie haunted castle
one spooky, dark night.

Alex Williams (7)
Ysgol Gynradd Wirfoddol Myfenydd, Llanrhystud

Best Friends

My friends are nice and cheerful like rainbows,
We never fall out like mums and children do.
They let me go to their wild parties.
I care about them.
We help each other just like teachers help us.
We love shopping, bags of fashion,
Giggling all the time.
Cups of coffee,
Lots of chatting,
Bestest friends forever,
That's us.

Catherine Nicole Richards (8)
Ysgol Gynradd Wirfoddol Myfenydd, Llanrhystud

Ghost Train

In the evil night, on the cranky train,
'Boo!' said a scary skeleton.
A vampire from his box corners me.
'Wooo!'
A ghost appearing right in front of me
Like a door slamming in my face.
I'm scared of ghosts,
I'm like a cat,
With its back like hedgehog spikes,
Chased by a dog.
'Help! Help me!' I'm scared.
A toothless skeleton pirate is having a sword fight,
Please tell me it's a dream.
An exit light flashes in my eyes,
I jump from the train like a rabbit,
Yes, I'm out! Like a freed prisoner.
I'm not scared . . .
Until the next time.

Ioan Rees-Evans (8)
Ysgol Gynradd Wirfoddol Myfenydd, Llanrhystud